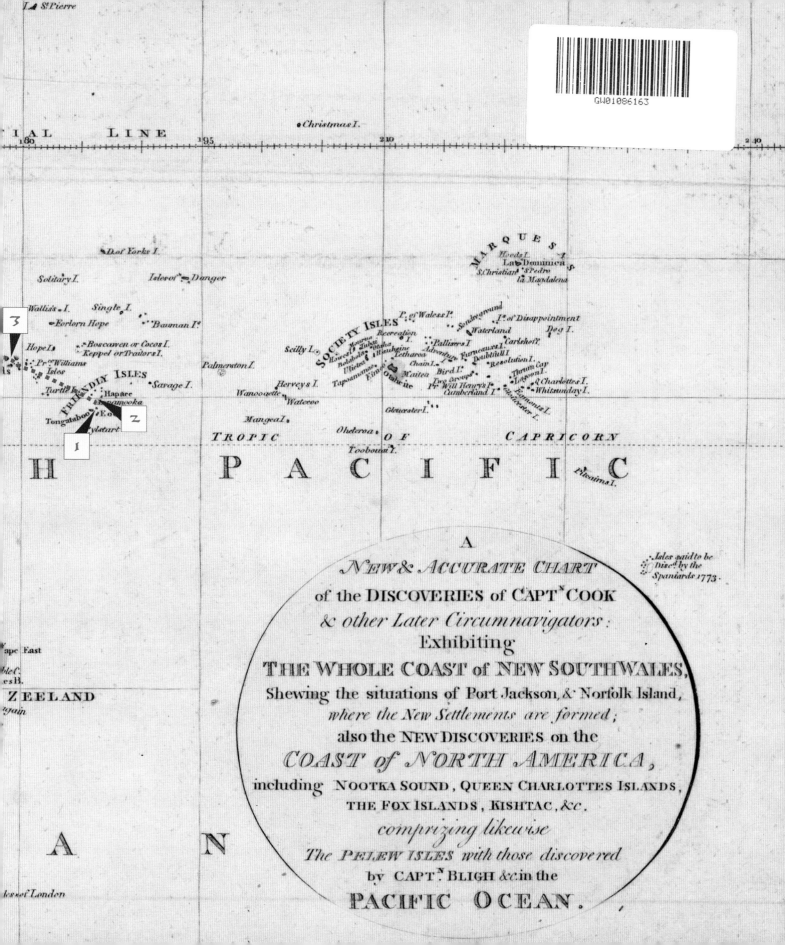

L. St Pierre

TIAL LINE   195   Christmas I.   210   240
180

D. of Yorks I.

MARQUESAS
Hoods I.
La Dominica
S. Christiana S. Pedro
la Magdalena

Solitary I.   Isles of Danger

Walliss I.   Single I.   P. of Waless I.   Sandy ground   I. of Disappointment
3   Waterland   Dog I.
Forlorn Hope   Bauman I.   SOCIETY ISLES Recreation
Hope I.   Boscaven or Cocos I.   Scilly L. Morina Recreation Pallisers I   Carlshoff
        Keppel or Traitors I.   Howeti Tabui Adventure I.   Furneaux I. Doubtlull I.
Pr. Williams   Bolabola Otaha   Letharoa   Chain I.   Resolution I.
Isles   Palmerston I.   Ulietea Huahine   Thrum Cap
                                                     Eimeo Maitea Bird I.   Lagoon I.
Turtle I.   Hapaee   Herveys I.   Tapoamanao Otaheite Two Groups   Q. Charlottes I.
FRIENDLY ISLES Annamooka   Wanooaette   Wateeoo   Pr. Will Henry's I. Egmonts I. Whitsunday I.
Tongataboo E. o   Savage I.   Cumberland I.
        Eylstart   Mangea I.   Gloucester I.
                      TROPIC   Oheteroa OF   CAPRICORN
2   Toobouai I.
1
H   P A C I F I C   Pitcairn I.

Isles said to be
Disc. by the
Spaniards 1773

A
NEW & ACCURATE CHART
of the DISCOVERIES of CAPT.ⁿ COOK
& other Later Circumnavigators:
Exhibiting
THE WHOLE COAST of NEW SOUTH WALES,
Shewing the situations of Port Jackson, & Norfolk Island,
where the New Settlements are formed;
also the NEW DISCOVERIES on the
COAST of NORTH AMERICA,
including NOOTKA SOUND, QUEEN CHARLOTTES ISLANDS,
THE FOX ISLANDS, KISHTAC, &c.
comprizing likewise
The PELEW ISLES with those discovered
by CAPT.ⁿ BLIGH &c. in the
PACIFIC OCEAN.

ape East

ble C.
es B.

ZEELAND

gain

A   N

es of London

IN
Bligh's
HAND

Surviving the Mutiny on the *Bounty*

Jennifer Gall

NATIONAL LIBRARY OF AUSTRALIA

Published by the National Library of Australia
Canberra ACT 2600
© National Library of Australia 2010

Text © Jennifer Gall

Foreword © Peter Cochrane

Books published by the National Library of Australia further the Library's objectives to interpret and highlight the Library's collections and to support the creative work of the nation's writers and researchers.

National Library of Australia Cataloguing-in-Publication entry

Author: Gall, Jennifer, 1959–

Title: In Bligh's hand : surviving the mutiny on the Bounty / by Jennifer Gall.

ISBN: 9780642277053 (pbk.)

Series: National Library of Australia collection highlights.

Subjects: Bligh, William, 1754-1817--Notebooks, sketchbooks, etc.

             Bligh, William, 1754-1817--Travel--Pacific Ocean.

             Bounty (Ship)

             Bounty Mutiny, 1789.

             Manuscripts, English--Facsimiles.

             Pacific Ocean--Description and travel.

Other Authors/Contributors:

             National Library of Australia.

Dewey Number: 910.92

Series concept development: Susan Hall
Editor: Joanna Karmel
Researchers: Maree Bentley and George Nichols
Pictures researcher: Felicity Harmey
Designer: Elizabeth Faul
Printed by Imago Australia Pty Ltd

The front and back cover images appear again on pages 74, 205, 32 and 49 respectively.
For full details, see the list of illustrations at the back of the book.

Foreword

In history, informed context is everything. Without it readers are lost as surely as they would be if they stepped into the Tardis and came out in Portsmouth or Paris in 1789.

So it is with one of the National Library's great treasures—William Bligh's notebook. This was Bligh's pocket record of the open-boat voyage from Tofua to Timor, following the mutiny on the *Bounty* on 28 April 1789. While the notebook's survival across centuries is a remarkable story in itself, the record of the voyage, across some 4000 miles of Pacific Ocean, is even more so.

In Bligh's Hand leads us through this astonishing text, enabling us to understand so much of what would otherwise be obscure or, perhaps, misunderstood. Jennifer Gall has matched her formidable subject in one crucial respect—she is as meticulous in taking us through the notebook and the voyage in the open boat as Bligh was meticulous in writing up the notebook and maintaining his little band of desperately hungry and exhausted loyalists. In doing so, the author enhances our understanding of the man and his company on this extraordinary journey—of his untiring sense of duty, his unfailing ambition and his commitment to extending the frontiers of British exploration and science; of his qualities as a leader and as a human being, and of his day-to-day record in the notebook—what that record tells us, its meanings, its biases and its silences.

In Bligh's Hand really opens the notebook to us. We see Bligh *in extremis* and, perhaps, in his finest moment. We see a leader who defies an ocean, whose fanatical attention to detail and procedure, along with his scrupulous fairness in the rationing of food, saves both him and his men—and, of course, his sea-splashed, pocket record of the journey.

Peter Cochrane

Contents

Editor's Notes

In this book, most chapters open with an extract from Bligh's notebook, acting as lead-ins to the chapter themes. A transcription appears adjacent to the facsimile of a page from the notebook. In a number of chapters, the transcript accompanying the facsimile page includes entries before and/or after the page shown. A symbol of a cutlass on the transcripts indicates where the text for the facsimile page begins.

A facsimile and transcript of the list of mutineers is reproduced in full at the back of the book. Bligh's entire notebook and the list of mutineers can be seen online at http://nla.gov.au/nla.ms-ms5393.

The transcripts of the notebook and the list of mutineers have been taken from *The Bligh Notebook: 'Rough Account—Lieutenant Wm Bligh's Voyage in the* Bounty's *Launch from the Ship to Tofua & from Thence to Timor', 28 April to 14 June 1789, with a Draft List of the* Bounty *Mutineers* edited by John Bach (National Library of Australia, 1986) and reviewed by George Nichols in 2010. Much of the information in the chapter on Bligh's navigational skills is sourced from this same book.

The spelling, punctuation and grammar that appear in quoted material have been retained. However, superscripts have been removed in all quoted material except for those in the transcripts opposite the facsimile pages. Bligh's crossings out have also been omitted. His insertions have not been shown as such but have been incorporated as part of the text. In quoted material, explanations for terms or missing words have been inserted in square brackets, where necessary.

Note that spellings of some of the *Bounty* crew members' names vary between publications about the mutiny.

Imperial measurements have been retained throughout the book in keeping with the times.

The story behind
William Bligh's notebook

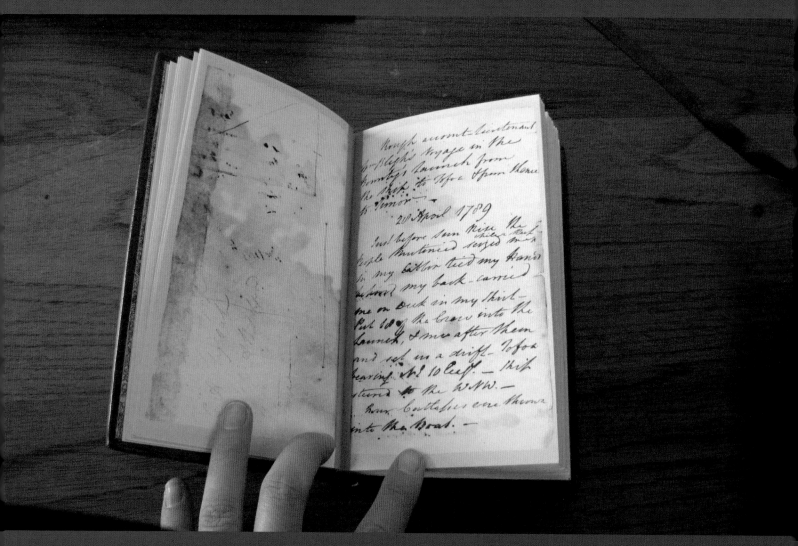

William Bligh's notebook, written onboard the *Bounty* launch, 1789

The notebook

This account was kept in my bosom as a common memorandum of our time & transposed into my fair Journal every day when the Weather would admit with every material circumstance which passed.—

Wm Bligh

Late in 1976, the National Library of Australia bid successfully at an auction in London to acquire a small leather-bound, water-stained pocket notebook of 107 pages, along with a map on a large sheet folded into the notebook titled 'Eye Sketch of Part of New Holland', and three loose sheets, folded into four, bearing descriptions of the mutineers. The book had remained in the possession of the Bligh family and its descendants for 187 years, until the time of sale. A special Commonwealth Government grant met the purchase price of $73 000—at that time a large sum of money—reflecting the great historical significance of the manuscript. Within the stained and blotted pages was preserved, in Lieutenant William Bligh's handwriting, the record of the 18 men cast adrift with him in a 23-foot open boat as a result of a mutiny on the *Bounty*, led by Fletcher Christian, during a voyage, the aim of which was to transplant breadfruit trees from Tahiti (then called Otaheiti) to the West Indies.

Perhaps most valuable of all was the notebook's potential to shed new light on Bligh's character, which would assist scholars in understanding why the mutiny occurred. The meticulous documentation of the voyage provided evidence of the regime Bligh put in place to enable him to sail the boat from Tofua (called Tofoa by Bligh), a volcanic island in the Tonga group, to Timor. The significance of the notebook was stated in the auction catalogue:

> *With its closely written pages of navigational recordings and reckoning, rough sketch charts and notes, the Bligh pocketbook provides the most complete navigational account yet known of the 3,500 mile voyage of the* Bounty's *launch from Tofua to Timor.*

The notebook was in fact not originally Bligh's possession. When he set sail in the launch, he had with him the official ship's log and fair journal, but he needed a small book for navigational calculations and notes throughout the often rough passage. These observations he would then rewrite into neater versions in the other volumes when the weather was calm. Bligh claimed the notebook from midshipman Thomas Hayward, who had used it as a signal book on the *Bounty*:

> *It happened that a Mr. Hayward had this Book with some Signals sat down in it wch appear in two Pages & I appropriated the blank leaves to this use.*

This logline has an hourglass beside it, unlike the one on the launch; the men had to learn to count accurately in seconds

Close analysis of the physical characteristics of the notebook has revealed that the book seems to have been bound in leather not long after Bligh returned home, and the marbled endpapers and blank end leaves also date from the time of binding. The first and last leaves of the notebook are probably the original paper wrappers. An antique-laid, cotton-rag paper is the medium for the pages.

When writing his account, every inch of space was precious, so Bligh did not leave margins. This meant that when the volume was bound, any writing close to the spine was drawn into the sewing of the sections. While some markings in the notebook were made in pencil, most of the entries are in ink, which was probably carried in a pocket writing case, and the sound quality of the pigment has ensured that the text is in excellent condition given its exposure to wind, salt and water. John Bach, editor of the 1986 scholarly edition of Bligh's notebook, has pointed out that Bligh had no intention of sharing his paper and ink with the *Bounty*'s master, John Fryer, who was anxious to maintain his own account of the voyage in the launch. This behaviour reveals much about Bligh's character, suggesting a controlling temperament and a man who feared further challenges to his authority.

There is a transition from Bligh's initial style of continuous narrative describing events from the mutiny on 28 April to noon on 7 May, at which point the notebook changes to that of a conventional log, with five columns on the left of a daily page for the hourly recording of the course, speed and wind conditions, and the remainder of the page for brief remarks. This change of format resulted from Bligh's successful creation on 5 May of a logline (a knotted cord of determined length that runs out from a reel to a piece of wood attached to it), which enabled him to measure the distances the launch covered. Using the logline, and having instructed the crew on how to count in seconds accurately, Bligh could calculate the correct speed of the launch through the water at regular intervals (see pages 86 and 105–107).

Obsessed with order, Bligh set aside one or more pages ahead of an entry for the quick, slightly untidy, mathematical calculations necessary to maintain course. Most of these calculations are dated and it is easy to link them to the relevant entry in the log. After the arrival of the launch on the coast of New Holland on 28 May, the notebook entries for each day take on the form of journal entries, with a page or more devoted to descriptions of the environment and the day's events.

The many contemporary descriptions of the mutiny are based predominantly on two accounts—that of Fryer, the master, who accompanied Bligh in the launch, and that of James Morrison, boatswain's mate, who remained with the *Bounty*. Morrison was later captured, sentenced to death and finally pardoned. Other accounts are based on evidence presented at the mutineers' court martial.

Looking at the water stains on the pages and reading the bleak descriptions of the sailors catching sea birds to dismember and eat raw, the modern reader can vividly imagine the cramped and desperate adventure of Bligh and his faithful mariners. We cannot help but marvel that, despite the rough and filthy conditions, the erratic motion of a boat running wildly before the trade winds and the buffetings of occasional squalls and storms, Bligh continued to write his regular, legible entries in the notebook, which survives for us to examine today.

The context

From 1760 to 1820, King George III reigned as a controversial monarch (although, due to his ill health, in the last 10 years of his reign his eldest son ruled as Prince Regent). On the one hand, the king was supremely cultivated and well educated, investing thousands of pounds in the Royal Academy, the Royal Botanical Gardens and the Royal Society to stimulate evolution of the arts and investigation of the sciences. On the other hand, he has been accused by historians of vindictively prolonging the war with the American rebels, trusting in the privations of extended conflict to reduce the rebels to penitence and contrition. His later madness added to the contradictions in perceptions of the achievements of his rule. Throughout George's reign, England began the process of industrialisation, laying the foundations for its status as the richest country in the world, dismantling many philosophical and humanitarian ideals in the process.

Paralleling eighteenth-century industrial innovation and economic revolution was the expansion of British naval exploration. The most famous voyages of discovery in the eighteenth century were those of James Cook, with whom Bligh served on Cook's third and final voyage. Within 10 years of setting forth, Cook's discoveries had completely transformed European knowledge of the Pacific region and paved the way for developing commerce and colonisation. Also playing a key role in maintaining George III's interest in the Pacific region was Joseph Banks, who sailed with Cook as botanist, as Banks had large holdings in the West Indies.

King George III, Queen
Charlotte and their six
oldest children, 1771

The eighteenth century was an era of immense political, economic, philosophical and social change on a global scale. The Jacobite Rebellion, the French Revolution, the American War of Independence and the Napoleonic Wars were momentous conflicts founded on the organisation of massed 'common' people opposing what they perceived as tyrannical rule by an artificial 'elite'. Massive population displacement occurred as a result of the industrial and economic revolutions, with rural workers seeking employment in urban mills and factories. In places such as the West Indies, slavery was condoned by the British as a means to run plantations profitably. It was an era of supreme unease, often referred to in the history of philosophy as the Enlightenment, where traditional power structures, institutions, moral codes and behaviours were under interrogation.

In this climate, the spirit of exploration and inquiry of the eighteenth-century voyages of discovery was increasingly controlled by the navy, under Admiralty orders, for military and strategic ends. Supplied by a series of colonial trading posts, British warships controlled the sea lanes to the Indian Ocean and the Far East, cruised the Atlantic to the American colonies and the West Indies, and patrolled the Mediterranean and the North Sea. Naval explorers like Cook and Bligh were defending British possessions in anticipation of extending control into new territory.

The mutiny on the *Bounty* has been described as a microcosm of the unrest in the emerging British Empire at that time, an allegory for the turmoil within power structures as the American War of Independence challenged the supremacy of British military and naval authority. Facing hostile French, Dutch and Spanish fleets, the British fought for and lost possession of the American colonies but, in the closing stages of the war, managed to win a series of engagements in the Channel and in the Caribbean, most notably at the Battle of the Saints in 1782.

Mirroring the vicissitudes of fortune, Bligh lost command of the *Bounty*, but he went on to play a heroic role in the Napoleonic Wars, to be commended by Admiral Horatio Nelson for his gallantry at the Battle of Copenhagen in 1801, and to end his career as a vice-admiral.

Fletcher Christian, who led the rebellion on the *Bounty*, was an educated man, descended from Manx gentry. He defied the established order of British naval authority by disputing Bligh's command and deposing him. The mutiny reverberates through history because it represented a fundamental question: can the overthrow of authority be justified by an appeal to natural justice? Debate still continues about whether Bligh's command really was tyrannical, or whether Christian's melancholic temperament simply meant that he was emotionally unable to endure serving his allotted term at sea on the *Bounty*. Christian was contemplating putting out to sea on a raft, so desperate was he to escape from what he described as Bligh's brutish behaviour, when midshipman Edward Young confided that Christian had the sympathy of several of the crew and that they would help him to take the ship. The mutiny was chaotic and brief, with few of the crew understanding what was really happening and many uncertain about to whom they should pledge allegiance.

Christian's mental torment is documented in his constant refrain of 'I am in hell', a phrase remembered by witnesses, and the generous provisions he provided for the men in the launch are evidence of his indecision. While he sought to be rid of Bligh's abrasive command, he definitely did not want the launch party to die. It appears that he acted in irrational desperation. Richard Ormond, director of the National Maritime Museum, Greenwich, has studied the evidence of court-martial records and naval documents to conclude that, while Bligh was an outstanding navigator and experienced sailor, he was unfortunately also 'over-zealous, a martinet and disciplinarian, with a blinkered view of human nature that flawed him as a commander'. Perhaps, however, the truth is closer to the idea proposed by Greg Dening in his 1992 book, *Mr Bligh's Bad Language*, in which he portrays Bligh as a consummate seaman who simply did not have the emotional intelligence or experience in 1789 to know how to play his role as commander on a complicated naval mission in which the challenge was not the usual physical and strategic challenge of fighting the French.

The purpose of the voyage

Breadfruit, possibly painted by Sydney Parkinson, 1769?

Bligh's voyage on the *Bounty* represented the next stage of naval enterprise, building on Cook's voyages of discovery in the Pacific. It was the first commercial voyage to the South Pacific and the motives were strategic rather than exploratory. Under Bligh's command, the *Bounty* was to transport breadfruit plants from Tahiti to the West Indies as a new, cheap food source for the plantation slaves there. The importance of breadfruit to the events of the mutiny cannot be overstated. For 200 years prior to the *Bounty*'s voyage, Europeans had known of this tree and declared it remarkable. First knowledge of the plant had come with the voyage of Alvaro de Mendana de Neyra in 1595 in which de Quiros was chief pilot. In 1686, William Dampier became the first European who recognised the breadfruit's food value and who detailed the various ways in which it could be prepared for the table. While Cook and Banks were impressed with the value of the breadfruit as a native fruit when they visited Tahiti in 1769, Cook was not enamoured of its flavour, describing it as being 'as disagreeable as that of a pickled olive' and 'its taste is insipid with a slight sweetness somewhat resembling that of the crumb of wheaten bread mixed with a Jerusalem artichoke'.

In contrast, Daniel Solander, botanist with Cook, wrote on 4 May 1776 to John Ellis, merchant, naturalist and king's agent, describing tasting breadfruit:

> [it] was by us during several months, daily eaten as a substitute for Bread, was universally esteemed as palatable and nourishing as Bread itself ... from the health

Above: Breadfruit

Left: Bligh, commander of the *Providence* and her tender *Assistant*, collecting breadfruit trees in his second, but this time successful, mission to transfer breadfruit from Tahiti to the West Indies, 1791–1793

& strength of whole nations whose principal food it is, I didn't scruple to call it one of the most usefull vegetables in the world ... As it undoubtedly must be of the utmost consequence to bring so valuable a Fruit to countrys where the climate is favorable to encourage every body who goes to any part of the world where it is to be met with, to bring it over.

There was a great incentive to introduce breadfruit to the West Indies, where slaves who worked the English sugar plantations were often short of food when hurricanes wiped out banana crops or yam crops failed. The islands were dependent for bread on the importation of expensive corn from the American mainland and, after the loss of the North American colonies, it was an even more attractive proposition to find an alternative food staple that could be grown in the West Indies.

Breadfruit trees are 30 to 60 feet (nine to 18 metres) in height with large, dark green, leathery leaves. The fruits are round, four to eight inches (10 to 20 centimetres) in diameter with green to brownish green skin. The inside is a white, fibrous pulp that cannot be eaten raw. Traditionally, breadfruit was baked in ground ovens or roasted in the coals of cooking fires. It is now most often eaten fried or steamed.

There were two men who were associated with instigating the scheme to transplant the breadfruit from Tahiti to the West Indies: Valentine Morris and Hinton East. Morris, who was appointed lieutenant-governor of St Vincent, an island in the Caribbean, in 1772, suggested to his friend, Joseph Banks, that the breadfruit would be an excellent answer to the problem of food shortages in the West Indies. East, a planter in Jamaica, was renowned for his impressive gardens in Kingston, and a constant correspondent with Banks. In a letter dated July 1784, he wrote that transplanting breadfruit would be 'of infinite importance to the West Indian Islands, in affording a wholesome and pleasant food to our Negroes … and not be subject to the danger of strong winds'. Banks, who had extensive plantations in the West Indies, heartily approved of the scheme and found a suitable opportunity to raise the matter with the king, who immediately gave orders to prepare for an expedition.

Finding a suitable vessel to transport breadfruit plants was the next challenge. Propagation is achieved through transplanting shoots, as the species does not seed, and it was this property of the breadfruit plant that was a major factor in the conditions onboard the *Bounty* that led to the discomfort and mounting aggression of the crew. However, in these early days of enthusiastic preparation, there were no premonitions of the disastrous outcome of the venture. It was necessary to find a vessel that was small and yet able to accommodate hundreds of breadfruit plants as well as the crew. Warships were out of the question as they were considered too cramped, so the Admiralty searched for a suitable merchant vessel. Six ships were identified as contenders and the *Bethia*, which at one time belonged to the family of Elizabeth Bligh, was chosen and renamed the *Bounty*. On 16 August 1787, Elizabeth's husband, William, was chosen to command the expedition. Bligh was extremely gratified at the appointment as it was a chance to both prove his worth to make money and to move towards promotion. At 33 years of age, he wrote a grateful letter to his mentor, Sir Joseph Banks:

> *I arrived yesterday from Jamaica and should have instantly paid my respects to you had not Mr. Campbell told me you were not to return from the Country untill Thursday. I have heard the flattering News of your great goodness to me, intending to honor me with the Command of the Vessel which you propose to go to the South Seas, for which, after offering you my most gratefull thanks, I can only assure you I shall endeavor and*

BOUNTY

"Sea Ruffians"

The *Bounty*

Bligh as a young midshipman in the 1770s

I hope succeed in deserving such a trust. I await your commands and am with the sincerest respect ...

Perseverance and dedication to duty were certainly qualities possessed by Bligh. Despite the mutiny and the drastic consequences, he was honourably acquitted after the court martial. In 1791, he was given command of the *Providence* and accomplished the transfer of breadfruit from Tahiti to the West Indies.

William Bligh's life and career

William Bligh was born into an old Cornish family on 9 September 1754, probably in Plymouth. This was the St Tudy branch of the family, which had settled in the area in 1619. They were regarded through the generations as well-to-do and learned, with the men entering clerical, legal, naval and civil service careers. Jane Pearce, a widow, married Francis Bligh, boatman and land waiter (customs official), who has been described as a 'much married man'. In 1754, the couple had a son, William. Jane died when William was about 14 and Francis died at the age of 59 in 1780. There was a half-sister, Catherine Pearce, from Jane's first marriage, and there are hints that Bligh may have visited her whenever he returned home from sea.

The first entry in Admiralty records for William Bligh occurs on 1 July 1762, when he is listed as 'servant' to Captain Keith Stewart of HMS *Monmouth*—at the age of seven years and nine months. This appointment at such an early age was a common procedure, enabling young men hopeful of a naval career to begin notching up their requisite six years of naval service so they could be ready for promotion to a naval lieutenancy at the earliest opportunity. Two of these years of service had to be conducted as midshipman or mate. Writing in 1899,

Sir William Laird Clowes, British journalist and historian, reminisces that:

> *It became a common practice to bear upon a ships books young gentlemen who, besides being much under eleven years of age, were still in the nursery at home, or were at school; and to bear nominally as seamen—boys, or as working servants—and to the prejudice of those classes—youngsters who were designed for the quarter-deck.*

There was ample provision for officers to have a large number of servants onboard, ranging from 50 in the case of Admiral of the Fleet, four for captains and one or two for lieutenants, masters, pursers, surgeons, chaplains, cooks, boatswains, gunners and carpenters. Not all of these servants were young men training for a naval career; barbers, footmen, tailors, fiddlers and artists followed their patrons to sea.

Captain James Cook meeting with Aboriginal men in Van Diemen's Land, 1777

Bligh's name next appears in 1770, on 27 July, on the pay sheets of HMS *Hunter*, a small 10-gun sloop. Although he is entered only as 'able seaman', he served in gun rooms, messed with the midshipman, and took his rightful place on the quarterdeck in anticipation of promotion. Bligh's name appears again in 1771 on the *Hunter*, but this time promoted to midshipman, a position he also filled on the HMS *Crescent* later that year. A term on the *Ranger* in 1774 preceded his momentous appointment as master of HMS *Resolution*, commanded by Captain James Cook. The voyage on the *Resolution* would prove fateful for Cook, who was speared to death in Hawaii. Cook had a high opinion of Bligh's skills as a cartographer and navigator, identifying him as a young officer who 'under my direction could be usefully employed in constructing charts, in taking views of the coasts and headlands near which we should pass, and in drawing plans of the bays and harbours in which we should anchor'. Perhaps, most importantly, Cook realised that competent fulfilment of these duties was 'wholly requisite if we would render our discoveries profitable to future navigators'.

The purpose of Cook's voyage was to seek a passage around the northern coast of America and to find a better way to the Pacific than via the Cape of Good Hope or around Cape Horn. Bligh performed many excursions to map and explore the coastline on the voyage and was recognised with an island being named Bligh's Cap on 24 December 1776. In January 1777, Bligh landed at Adventure Bay, Van Diemen's Land, an area he explored thoroughly. A year later, the expedition discovered the Sandwich Islands and Bligh conducted a survey of the new territory.

Cook's last entries in his ship's journal and the journal he was preparing for publication both mention Bligh, indicating the position of responsibility the master had assumed. On 17 January, he wrote in his final journal entry a description of his intentions that led to his death:

In the evening Mr. Bligh returned, and reported, that he had found a bay in which was good anchorage, and fresh water ... I resolved to carry the ships, there to refit, and supply ourselves with every refreshment that the place could afford.

In the attacks following Cook's death, Bligh displayed courage and initiative in leading his party to safety after retrieving most of the *Resolution's* sails that were lying on the beach awaiting repair. On the homeward voyage, Bligh continued to map the uncharted coastline, reaching England on 4 October 1780, after being away for more than four years. He was paid off and quite probably spent some time assisting with the publication of Cook's journal, contributing several plans and charts. Comments written in the margin of Bligh's copy of Captain James King's commentary in the published edition of Cook's journal of the fateful voyage are often angry, and dispute the veracity of King's account.

During a holiday on the Isle of Man in the 1770s, Bligh met the Christian family—an occurrence that was to have lasting repercussions. A more harmonious and enduring relationship for Bligh than the one that transpired with Fletcher Christian was formalised on 4 February 1781, at Onchan, near Douglas, on the Isle of Man, when he married Elizabeth Betham of Onchan, a descendant on her mother's side of the notable Campbell family. Bligh took great pleasure in setting up house with his wife when they finally bought a home in May 1783, and his comments convey this contentment:

Since May Mrs Bligh and I have begun housekeeping, and find it a most agreeable change from lodgings. We have one of the neatest houses in Town for eight guineas a year and have with little trouble furnished it decently.

Bligh saw his first naval battle as master of the *Belle Poule*, at the Dogger Bank in August 1781. His next significant action was on the *Cambridge*, taking part in the relief of Gibraltar between 1782 and 1783. With the end of the American War of Independence, the navy was immediately reduced to half pay and Bligh consequently accepted employment as commander of a merchant vessel, the *Lynx*, owned by his wife's uncle, Duncan Campbell. A surviving letter from 1787 records that Bligh was in charge of the *Britannia*, and that onboard was a young man named Fletcher Christian. Another letter, written by Captain Taubman, requests a position for Christian. After Bligh replied that there was no vacancy, Christian himself wrote that he wished only to learn his profession and was content to join the ship as foremast-man. Bligh agreed to his proposal. At the voyage's end, Christian was full of praise for Bligh's kindness, but remarked that the commander was a passionate man and implied that he had some ability to calm Bligh when he became agitated. On the following voyage, Christian went as the commander's second mate. However, the

Bligh's wife, Elizabeth, 1782

subsequent voyage together on the *Bounty* was not to be so smooth. An acerbic comment on Christian's aptitude for a naval career is found in a letter written to Bligh by Captain Edward Lamb, commander of the *Adventure*, in the Jamaica trade:

> *When we got to sea and I saw your partiality for the young man, I gave him every advice and information in my power, though he went about every point of duty with a degree of indifference that to me was truly unpleasant.*

Who possessed the less disciplined temperament of the two seamen? As the story underlying Bligh's notebook unfolds, so does the complex set of vexations that weighed upon both men.

'Just before Sun Rise
the People Mutinied'

The mutiny

Rough account — Lieutenant
Wm Bligh's Voyage in the
Bounty's Launch from
the Ship to Tofoa & from thence
to Timor —

28 April 1789

Just before Sun Rise the
People Mutinied seized me while in
in my Cabbin tied my Hands
behind my back — carried
me on Deck in my Shirt —
Put 18 of the Crew into the
Launch, & me after them
and set us a drift — Tofoa
bearing NE 10 leag.s — Ship
steered to the WNW —
four Cutlasses were thrown
into the Boat. —

This account was kept in my bosom as a common memorandum of our time & transposed into my fair Journal every day when the Weather would admit with every material circumstance which passed.—

Wm Bligh

It happened that a Mr Hayward had this Book with some Signals sat down in it wch appear in two Pages & I appropriated the blank leaves to this use.

Rough account—Lieutenant Wm Bligh's Voyage in the Bounty's Launch from the Ship to Tofoa & from thence to Timor—

28 *April* 1789

Just before Sun Rise the People Mutinied seized me while asleep in my Cabbin tied my Hands behind my back—carried me on Deck in my Shirt— Put 18 of the Crew into the Launch, & me after them and set us a drift— Tofoa bearing NE 10 leag^s—Ship steered to the WNW.—

Four Cutlasses were thrown into the Boat.—

The Pirates seizing Capt.ⁿ Bligh.

Why has the mutiny on the *Bounty* remained so popular as a field of historical research? Looking at a selection of the vast number of publications on the topic, dating from the time of Bligh's return to England to the present, it is readily apparent that authors have taken sides and constructed cases according to which man they deemed to be the guilty party—the commander, William Bligh, or the master's mate, Fletcher Christian. Recent scholarship documenting the voyage of the *Bounty* has taken a broader view, with the mutiny being considered as the result of many contributing factors, not just a clash of personalities between the two men. It is more instructive to re-imagine life onboard the *Bounty*, and how relationships functioned between the crew, those in command, and the Tahitians, who played such an important part in the way in which the mutiny and its aftermath evolved.

William Bligh as commander must be examined to determine what he hoped to achieve on the voyage. Oddly enough, one of the best clues about how Bligh saw himself and how he wished to be remembered throughout history exists in his choice of burial place. Bligh's body is interred in the churchyard of St Mary's, Lambeth, in what are now the grounds of the Museum of Garden History. On top of his fine stone tomb is a breadfruit. The grave is near those of the famous father and son, John Tradescant the elder and the younger, who, from the late sixteenth to the late seventeenth century, collected exotic plants from around the world, making a lasting impression on the nature of English gardening.

Bligh carried out his horticultural experiments in the reverse order of the Tradescants, by planting English fruit and vegetables in various locations on his travels. In 1788, when Bligh

Bligh's patron, the Right Hon. Sir Joseph Banks

The mutineers seizing Bligh on the *Bounty*

Bligh's tombstone, St Mary's, Lambeth, London, features a breadfruit

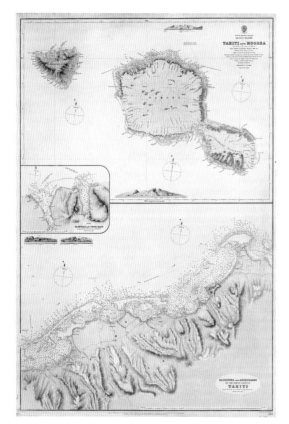

An 1880 chart showing Tahiti, part of the Society Islands, from where Bligh collected breadfruit trees on his voyage in the *Bounty*

anchored in Adventure Bay on Bruny Island, Van Diemen's Land, he and his crew planted fruit trees and vegetables and recorded friendly meetings with the Aboriginal people, before heading to Tahiti. Bligh returned in 1792 to discover that of his entire plantings only one apple tree remained, but his interest in botanical subjects and his desire to document natural history observations endured throughout his Pacific voyages. In St Mary's churchyard, Bligh is acknowledged on his tomb as both a man of science and an esteemed naval commander.

Bligh had served as master on Cook's third and fatal voyage to the Pacific on the *Resolution*. We know from Bligh's annotations in the margins of Cook's account, *A Voyage to the Pacific Ocean* (1784), now held in the Admiralty Library, Greenwich, that he was angry about the inadequate acknowledgment of his contribution to the mapping and surveying that he had conducted on the voyage. Being overlooked on this occasion fuelled Bligh's ambitions to conduct his own expedition and to make a contribution to scientific and navigational knowledge that could not be ignored.

Fortune smiled on Bligh in providing Joseph Banks as a patron. It was flattering for Bligh to be invited to discuss botanical, nautical and shipboard health matters with Banks in preparation for the *Bounty* voyage, and it appears that he was determined to outdo Cook's achievements on every count, particularly as a humane captain. Historian Greg Dening has demonstrated through statistical analysis that, in this era, Bligh used the lash least of any naval commander in the Pacific. Log records show that he was determined to run a clean and civilised ship, where harsh punishment was the last resort in maintaining discipline. When he was forced to give Matthew Quintal two dozen lashes for 'insolence and contempt', Bligh wrote in the log that 'until this afternoon I had hoped I could have performed the voyage without punishment to anyone'. This event was four months into the voyage. Was such a hope naive or idealistic? However it is judged, the comment certainly demonstrates the way in which he deliberated over issues, perhaps too much, to reach a decision that was just. Some have argued that Bligh was too soft, that his reluctance to use the lash undermined the institutional codes which gave meaning to the daily grind of shipboard duties.

Under Banks' patronage, Bligh's loyalties were divided between the Admiralty's directive to transport breadfruit plants and its strategic response to French naval activity in the region. Other competing priorities were Banks' scientific requests and Bligh's own humanitarian ideals as he tried to implement hygienic and moral experiments onboard. These mixed motives for the naval vessel's voyage and Bligh's leniency, which could have been interpreted as weakness, created an ambiguity that was unfamiliar and discomforting to the sailors.

The Admiralty at this time did not share Bligh's idealism or his ambitions. It responded in the least expensive way possible to the powerful plantation owners' lobby by providing the cheapest vessel and the minimum number of seamen to transplant the breadfruit. Bligh's superhuman efforts to speedily prepare the inadequately small *Bounty* in order to depart in time to catch the best weather of the season were thwarted by the Admiralty's failure to send his orders to sail. By delaying his departure, he missed the opportunity to round Cape Horn and, compounding the setback, missed the fair winds that would blow the ship through Endeavour Straits on their return journey from Tahiti. This tardiness of Admiralty officers was more damaging to Bligh's ambitions than any behaviour by the general crew. As a consequence of the delay, the *Bounty* was forced to shelter for the hurricane season and the crew lived long enough with the Tahitians to begin to feel that they were part of the islanders' society.

A problem with the division of labour on the ship was the imbalance of skilled and unskilled seamen. Amongst the 46 crew, there were only 10 able seamen upon whom completing the difficult and skilled daily tasks of sailing relied. When the weather was bad, these 10 were on watch constantly and this bound the group together, united in discontent. Bligh felt unsupported in his command and, following the mutiny, conveys his sense of betrayal in a letter to his wife:

> *I had not sufficient Officers & had they granted me Marines most likely the affair would never have happened—I had not a Spirited & brave fellow about me.*

Bligh took a substantial cut in annual salary, from £500 to £50, to command the *Bounty*, so eager was he to make his mark on a Pacific expedition. However, he was acutely aware of the importance of making money for his own security and took on the added strain as purser on the voyage. To protect his investment in provisions, Bligh kept track of every morsel of

John Adams, who was known as Alexander Smith at the time of the mutiny

food and drink consumed or pilfered by the crew. Adding to this financial strain was an incident recounted years after the uprising by John Adams, the sole survivor of Christian's mutineers able to be questioned some years later. Adams stated that an issue about money had arisen between Bligh and Christian at the Cape of Good Hope. It has been suggested that Bligh lent Christian money in a complicated arrangement that meant Christian was borrowing against wages he did not yet possess and was effectively in debt to two parties. Thus both men were stretched to their limits financially and Christian was feeling trapped both economically and physically by his commander. Because of connections between their two families, he felt he was Bligh's equal in education, breeding and social rank, but the naval hierarchy determined that he must remain subservient, and this he could not endure. Christian's conviction of powerlessness was probably more destructive than the superficial claim that he had 'been in hell for weeks past' because of Bligh's aggressive temper and verbal abuse. It has been well established that Bligh was not physically violent and that he was lenient in his use of the lash. However, three times in his career he failed to read the warning signs of intense dissatisfaction in the behaviour of his subordinates and thus experienced rebellion triggered by blinkered adherence to his perceived duty.

From his writings, it is evident that Bligh was particularly interested in conducting a model expedition; one in which his crew's physical health would be carefully maintained, and their mental wellbeing would be assisted by the inclusion of a fiddler, Michael Byrn, to provide music for dancing and entertainment. Bligh remarks in his log of 11 January 1788:

> I now Ordered my people to be at three Watches, and gave the Charge of the Third Watch to a Mr. Fletcher Christian one of my Mates. I have ever considered this among Seamen as Conducive to health, and not being Jaded by keeping on Deck every other four hours, it adds much to their Content and Chearfulness. Some time for relaxation and Mirth is absolutely necessary, and I have considered it so much so that after 4 oClock, the Evening is laid aside for their Amusement and dancing. I had great difficulty before I left England to get a Man to play the Violin and I prefered at last to take One two thirds Blind than come without one.

This was a well-intentioned but not a well-received idea. Alternative accounts of life aboard the *Bounty* record opposition to Bligh's dancing regime and possibly to the fact that the commander had appointed the musician, rather than allowing, as was the tradition, a fiddler and other musicians to emerge naturally from amongst the ranks.

Bligh's deep ambition was to provide meticulous natural history observations to add to the body of knowledge about the Pacific. The log entries, such as the one of 22 February, in which he notes these observations, provide some of his most considered writing; observations that reveal how Bligh first saw the beauty of a natural occurrence, then engaged his critical faculties to describe it:

> As most ships on advancing towards and near the line, so we [?] and the Sea becomes animated with numerous light spots occasioned by innumerable Marine Animals near the Surface that emit a Strong Sparkling light. There are a Variety of them, but the kind I now picked up were about 2 inches long and 1½ Inch in Circumference resembling very much a piece of vegetating coral, through the pores of which the light was emitted in distinct particles, that with the refractive medium of the water had a most powerful effect. They appeared totally inanimated, and their bulk consisted so much of aqueous matter, that in water very little remains as substance.

From our vantage point of hindsight, we can view Bligh as a scholar and an idealist determined to please the influential lobby of West Indian plantation owners by transporting the breadfruit plants from Tahiti, but equally committed to making naval and scientific discoveries and securing himself a promotion to captain. The crew of the *Bounty* had no such understanding of their commander, or any share in his focus to complete the mission. Dening provides an insightful description of Bligh's men and how they preserved their sense of order: 'To a sailor, the text of his life was in knowing every degree of the relationship of his wooden world to the wind and sea and land outside it and the relationship of every place, role and action within it to himself'. The language of seamen was a dialect that bound the crew and defined their identity, living as they did in perpetual movement, with constant danger, described by an English cleric of the time as 'numbered neither with the living nor the dead'. What happened in the Pacific as the crew waited three months in Tahiti for the weather to improve, according to Dening's hypothesis, was the decay of the boundaries and codes that provided the sailors with their identity. Caught between the life of the Tahitians and the uncertain destiny of the *Bounty* expedition, the resulting unease created a prevailing confusion that Christian shaped into a mutiny by removing Bligh and his ambitions from the scenario.

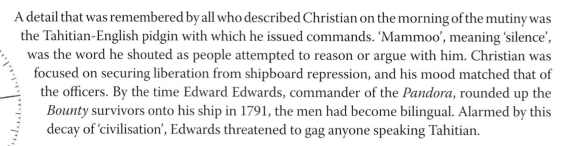

A detail that was remembered by all who described Christian on the morning of the mutiny was the Tahitian-English pidgin with which he issued commands. 'Mammoo', meaning 'silence', was the word he shouted as people attempted to reason or argue with him. Christian was focused on securing liberation from shipboard repression, and his mood matched that of the officers. By the time Edward Edwards, commander of the *Pandora*, rounded up the *Bounty* survivors onto his ship in 1791, the men had become bilingual. Alarmed by this decay of 'civilisation', Edwards threatened to gag anyone speaking Tahitian.

Ship's master John Fryer (who was forced into the launch with Bligh) and boatswain's mate James Morrison (who remained loyal to Bligh but stayed on the *Bounty*) wrote accounts of the events leading up to the mutiny which provide additional information to the account written by Bligh. On that morning, Bligh failed to appear on deck until noon, a most uncharacteristic omission suggesting that Bligh was severely incapacitated by some kind of physical affliction—dysentery perhaps or a severe migraine—an assertion without evidence. When he did appear, he was in a raging temper. Taking a turn about the quarterdeck, he discovered some coconuts that he had bought were missing. He was of the opinion that they could not have been stolen without the officers noticing. All of them denied knowledge of a theft, at which time, Morrison reports, Bligh proclaimed 'then you must have taken them yourselves' and questioned them individually. Christian answered the query with, 'I do not know Sir, but I hope you dont think me so mean as to be Guilty of Stealing yours'. Bligh responded:

> *Yes you dam'd Hound I do—You must have stolen them from me or you could give a better account of them—God dam you, you Scoundrels, you are all thieves alike, and combine with the men to rob me—I suppose you'll Steal my Yams next, but I'll sweat you for it, you rascals, I'll make half of you Jump overboard before you get through Endeavour Streights.*

Morrison continues his description:

> *The Cocoa Nuts were Carried aft, & He Went below, the officers then got together and were heard to murmur much at such treatment, and it was talked among the Men that the Yams would be next seized, as Lieut. Bligh knew that they had purchased large quantitys of them and set about secreting as many as they Could.*

XV.

Fruit du Cocotier.

Before leaving Tahiti, the *Bounty* crew bought a supply of coconuts for the next part of the voyage

Was Christian unfairly victimised? It seems from Morrison's description that in this instance all the officers felt threatened by Bligh. However, Morrison next records Christian's decision to act:

in the Morning of the 28th the Boatswain Came to my hammock and waked me telling me to my great surprize that the ship was taken by Mr. Christian.

Confusion and distress were rife, with the crew uncertain about what was happening and who to obey:

Mr. Hayward & Mr. Hallet begd with tears in their eyes to be sufferd to remain in the ship but Mr. Christian ordered them to be silent.

THE COCOA-NUT TREE.

An illustration of a coconut tree in the 1820 publication, *Dangerous Voyage of Captain Bligh in an Open Boat … in the Year 1789* by William Bligh

Fryer interceded and managed to negotiate that Bligh and his loyalists be placed in the launch rather than the small, dilapidated cutter. Something of Bligh's desperation, cloaked in his own account by his outrage, is revealed in the conversation reported by Morrison:

> when Mr. Bligh found that He must go, he beggd of Mr. Christian to desist, saying 'I'll Pawn my Honor, I'll Give My Bond, Mr. Christian, never to think of this if youll desist'; and urged his wife and family, to which Mr. Christian replyd 'No, Captain Bligh, if you had any Honor, things had not come to this; and if you Had any regard for your Wife & family, you should Have thought on them before, and not behaved so much like a villain'.

Morrison also notes that the officers never made 'the least attempt to rescue the ship which would have been effected had any attempt been made by one of them'. He remarks that although Christian had fewer men:

> none seemd Inclined to dispute the superiority and Mr. Christian at the Head of Eight or Nine Men was permitted to proceed … and even after the Boat was gone some of them hardly knew what part they had acted in the Business.

Morrison recounts Christian's description of his decision-making process leading to the mutiny, listing his cumulative hurt at Bligh's insults, his decision to quit the ship on a raft with a few supplies and head for Tofua, and the exchange with Mr Stewart, who woke Christian to relieve the watch and, finding him 'much out of order', begged him not to leave on the grounds that 'the People are ripe for any thing'. Gathering his supporters, securing weapons from the arms chest on the pretext of shooting a shark and arming his men (including those 'who stood in his way, without their knowing for what purpose'), Christian secured Bligh and his companions and set them adrift in the launch.

Christian's first act was to order the breadfruit trees to be thrown overboard, which took until the first or second of May. He then took possession of the commander's cabin.

From Bligh's perspective, his perfect expedition was subverted in the space of a few short hours. Writing in the launch in the notebook he requisitioned from Thomas Hayward, he notes on 28 April 1789:

> *Just before Sun Rise the People Mutinied seized me while asleep in my Cabbin tied my Hands behind my back—carried me on Deck in my Shirt—Put 18 of the Crew into the Launch, & me after them and set us a drift.*

Bligh later expanded this account when he had time to ponder events:

> *Just before sun-rising, while I was yet asleep, Mr. Christian, with the master at arms, gunner's mate, and Thomas Burket, seaman, came into my cabin, and seizing me, tied my hands with a cord behind my back, threatening me with instant death, if I spoke or made the least noise: I, however, called as loud as I could, in hopes of assistance; but they had already secured the officers who were not of their party, by placing centinels at their doors. There were three men at my cabin door, besides the four within; Christian had only a cutlass in his hand, the others had muskets and bayonets. I was hauled out of bed, and forced on deck in my shirt, suffering great pain from the tightness with which they had tied my hands. I demanded the reason of such violence, but received no other answer than abuse, for not holding my tongue. The master, the gunner, the surgeon, Mr. Elphinstone, master's mate, and Nelson, were kept confined below; and the fore hatchway was guarded by centinels. The boatswain and carpenter, and also the clerk, Mr. Samuel, were allowed to come upon deck, where they saw me standing abaft the mizen-mast, with my hands tied behind my back, under a guard, with Christian at their head …*
>
> *I asked for arms, but they laughed at me, and said I was well acquainted with the people among whom I was going, and therefore did not want them; four cutlasses, however, were thrown into the boat …*

A dogmatic interpretation of rules and a fiery temper had led Bligh into the mutiny on the *Bounty*, but the benefits of Bligh's stubborn adherence to regulations were revealed in the open launch when his meticulous attention to detail and regimental procedures in the face of appalling conditions kept his loyal supporters alive.

'Star tatowed on the left breast'

The protagonists

Fletcher Christian. Aged 24 Years — 5. 9. High [set in] Dark Swarthy Complexion

Complexion	Dark & very Swarthy
Hair	Blackish or very dark brown
Make	Strong
Marks	Star tatowed on the Left breast

and on the backside. — His knees
stands a little out, and may be called a little bow legged
He is subject to violent perspiration & particularly in
his hands so that he soils any thing he handles.

George Stewart — Aged 23 — 5. 7. High —

Complexion	Good
Hair	Dark
Make	Slender & narrow chested & long Neck

Marks — Star on the Left breast — one on the left Arm —
tatowed on the backside — & tattooed with Darts on the left
arm — Small face & black Eyes —

Peter Heywood — Aged 17 — 5. 7.

Complexion	Fair
Hair	Light brown
Make	Well proportioned
Marks	Very much Tattowed and on the Right

Leg is tattowed the Three legs of Man as that coin is
At this time he had not done growing — He speaks with the
Isle of Man accent

Edward Young — Aged 22. 5. 8. High

Complexion	Dark and rather a bad look
Hair	Dark brown
Make	Strong
Marks	Lost several of his fore teeth & those

that remain are all rotten. — A small mole on the
left side of the throat and on the right arm is tatowed
a heart & Dart through it with E Y underneath. and the
year 1788 or 1789

feet In

Fletcher Christian. Aged 24 Years—5 .. 9 High Dark Swarthy Complexion
Complexion ——————Dark & very swathy
Hair————————Blackish or very dark brown
Make————————Strong
Marks ———————Star tatowed on the left breast and tatowed on the
backside.—His knees stands a little out and may be called a little bow legged
He is subject to violent perspiration & particularly in His hands so that he
soils any thing he handles.

ft   In

George Stewart—Aged 23—5 .. 7—High—
Complexion ——————Good
Hair————————Dark
Make————————Slender & narrow chested & long kneck
Marks ———————Star on the left breast—one on the left Arm—
tatowed on the backside—A Heart with Darts on the left arm—Small face
& black Eyes.

f   in

Peter Haywood—Aged 17—5 .. 7
Complexion ——————Fair
Hair————————Light brown
Make————————well proportioned
Marks ———————Very much tattowed and on the Right Leg is tattowed
The Three legs of Man as that coin is. At this time he had not done
growing—He speaks with Strong Manks or I. of Man accent

f   in

Edward Young—Aged 22 .. 5 .. 8 High
Complexion ——————Dark and rather a bad look
Hair_____Dark brown
Make————————Strong
Marks ———————Lost several of his fore teeth & those that remain are
all rotten.—A small mole on the left side of the throat and on the right arm is
tatowed [a?] Heart & Dart through it with E . Y underneath. and the
[date of?] the year 1788 or 1789.

Bligh and 18 others being set adrift in the launch by the *Bounty* mutineers

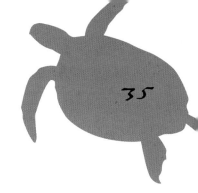

The list of mutineers

Bligh's list of mutineers contains careful physical descriptions of the men involved in the insurrection. His portrayal of Fletcher Christian is remarkable for the detail he provides about Christian's 'violent perspiration'. The rancour Bligh felt towards the leader of the mutiny is expressed in his claim that, because of these sweats, Christian 'soils any thing he handles'.

The intimate details of the men's tattoos and the attention given to describing their build or 'make' highlights the extraordinary level of personal knowledge Bligh retained of his crew. In his descriptions of injuries lies a record of hard lives served in dangerous conditions at sea: James Morrison had 'Lost the Use of the Upper Joint of the Fore Finger of the Right Hand'; Charles Churchill bore the disfigurement of 'a Severe Scald' on his left hand; William McCoy carried a scar 'where he has been Stabbed in the Belly'; and Thomas Burkitt had a fair complexion 'very much pitted with the Small Pox'—he survived this deadly disease only to have his life ended in a public execution as a result of the mutiny.

One of the most interesting categories included by Bligh is that of the mutineers' 'Marks'. Many of these were acquired by the men during their stay on Tahiti and were evidence of how the men had used indigenous techniques to administer their own designs onto their bodies. Christian is listed as possessing a 'Star tatowed on the left breast and tatowed on the backside', an observation suggesting that life at sea had little privacy. Young Peter Heywood had carved his Manx birthplace into his body with 'The Three legs of Man', the symbol of the Isle of Man.

There is evidence of dental disease due to poor diet and poor personal hygiene practices. Edward Young, aged 22, had 'Lost several of his fore teeth & those that remain are all rotten'. Charles Norman, carpenter's mate, must have been an alarming sight as Bligh notes that his face was 'pitted with the Small Pox' and that he had a 'Remarkable Motion with his head and eyes'.

A number of the men had language peculiarities. Henry Hilbrant was 'Hanoverian Born & Speaks Bad English', while John Williams was 'a Native of Guernsey & Speaks French'. Communication must have been difficult at times for these men. How much did they comprehend on the morning of the mutiny as Christian ranted and Bligh desperately attempted to negotiate with him?

'The Three legs of Man', the symbol for the Isle of Man that Peter Heywood had tattooed on his right leg

Reading through the names, Bligh's descriptions provide the details for our imagination to recreate these scarred and tattooed men of varying build and height. Fragments of their personality are reflected in their taste for tattoo designs, and we have a sense of men who had lived through brutality and horrible disease; of strong build or slight; of fair complexion or pock-marked; with dark or light hair. Ironically, given his determination to report their behaviour as the barbaric actions of a herd, Bligh's notes humanise the accused to show them as individuals. No longer are they merely an amorphous band of mutineers.

Fletcher Christian

At the heart of the events that led to the mutiny on the *Bounty* is the tortuous relationship between William Bligh and Fletcher Christian. Their association brought into conflict personal ideals of authority, leadership, etiquette and duty. At the beginning of the voyage, the two men were friends, having met on the Isle of Man, and Bligh had acted as a mentor for the advancement of Christian's naval career. Both men appear to have believed passionately in their own superior ability to command men. Christian's family had administered justice on the Isle of Man for over three centuries and Christian had developed his own ideas about leadership based on camaraderie and the use of democratic decision-making. In comparison, Bligh believed in himself as a self-made leader, a commander formed by the experiences of battles and possessing excellent navigations skills honed during a number of scientific voyages of exploration.

Christian, seventh child of Charles and Ann Christian, was born on 25 September 1764 at Moorland Close near the English Lake District. His father was a merchant and head of the Christian family of Milntown on the Isle of Man and of Ewanrigg in Cumbria. Records on the isle dating back to 1380 document Fletcher Christian's ancestors. For successive generations, the family had acted as mediators between the people of the isle and the English aristocrats, such as the earls of Derby, who functioned like the isle's uncrowned kings. The Christians were called 'First Deemsters', effectively judiciary heads administering the unwritten laws of the island. In this role, the family accumulated choice land and wielded power in political, legal, university and religious positions. They were influential in the administration of commercial ventures in India and the East and West Indies. Their dominance was strengthened by a large number of illegitimate relations, who, unlike their counterparts in notable English families, took their fathers' surname and further extended the family's power. Not just a complacent man of rank, John XVII,

St Bees, Whitehaven, Cumbria, where Fletcher Christian went to school

who had become the young head of the family in Fletcher's childhood, experimented with a number of revolutionary ideas aimed at providing benefits, such as delivering England's first free milk, to the wider population beyond his family.

Christian's mother, Ann Dixon, came from an old, established Cumbrian family. As a young boy, Christian attended the Cockermouth Free Grammar School. William Wordsworth, the poet, also went to the school at this time, although the two are unlikely to have known each other well because of their age disparity. After leaving Cockermouth, he proceeded, like his brothers, to St Bees School near Whitehaven, founded by Elizabeth I in 1583. Glynn Christian, biographer of Fletcher Christian and a direct descendant, describes his ancestor's education at St Bees as fitting for a young gentleman, with the following as his subjects: the catechism, Latin, Greek, mathematics and navigation. Had his father not died, Christian may well have continued to Cambridge in the centuries-old family tradition and never have sought a career in the navy. Unfortunately, the family fell into bankruptcy when

Christian was aged four, after imprudent investments by his brothers depleted the family fortune. With her daughter, Mary, and sons, Fletcher and Charles, Ann Christian moved to the Isle of Man. Fletcher Christian remained at school until 1782 and, at the age of 19, in April 1783, he signed on as midshipman to serve on HMS *Eurydice*, sailing to India. On the return voyage, the captain, George Courtney, made Christian an acting lieutenant and appointed him in charge of a watch. On this voyage, he was described as an officer who 'ruled over them in a superior, pleasant manner'.

A career in the navy offered the opportunity for Christian to redress his reduced prospects and rise to a position of influence, especially with the assistance of a sponsor—and this was the role assumed by Bligh. The husband of Christian's cousin, Dorothy, recommended that he serve directly under Bligh, and so the young sailor wrote requesting a place. Bligh responded that no officers' positions were available, but Fletcher replied, saying that wages were no object and that he only wished to learn his profession and, if Captain Bligh would allow him to mess with the gentlemen, he would readily enter the ship as a foremast-man until there was a vacancy amongst the officers. On their first voyage to the West Indies together on the *Britannia*, Bligh and Christian had a strong relationship as teacher and pupil, and the experience assured Bligh sufficiently to recommend the appointment of Christian to the *Bounty*. Christian signed on as master's mate. Perhaps this master/disciple relationship was the foundation of the later conflict; as Christian gained confidence and understandably wanted to assume more responsibility, Bligh might have been unable to allow him the freedom to assert his own judgment.

How did Christian appear to those who served with him on the *Bounty*? Charles Christian, in his unpublished autobiography, described his brother's impressive physical strength and wrote that he was 'full of professional Ambition and Hope'. He quoted his brother as remarking: 'I delight to set men an example. I not only can do every part of Common Sailor's Duty, but am upon a par with a principal part of the officers'.

The brothers met up while Fletcher waited for the *Bounty* to sail and after Charles, surgeon on the East Indiaman *Middlesex*, had returned from India. Significantly, the most interesting news exchanged by the brothers concerned the mutiny onboard the *Middlesex*, against the cruelty of Captain Rogers, in which Charles was one of the officers involved. In this case, Charles was not imprisoned because mutiny on a merchantman was not considered a crime against the king and, indeed, Rogers was punished equally with the officers who had mutinied against him. As he set sail onboard the *Bounty*, Fletcher would have been thinking about the duty of officers to mediate between the men and the commander, perhaps speculating on exactly how far such an intermediary could go to preserve what he considered to be justice.

Bligh's description of Christian after the mutiny is not at all flattering:

> *Master's mate, aged 24 years, 5 feet 9 inches high, blackish or very dark complexion, dark brown hair, strong made; a star tattooed on his left breast, tattooed on his backside; his knees a little out, and he may be called rather bow-legged. He is subject to violent perspirations, and particularly his hands, so that he soils anything he handles.*

Lawrence Lebogue, Christian's shipmate on the *Bounty*, recalled that his colleague always had a girl with him in Tahiti, as probably did most of the crew.

After the mutiny, Christian led his comrades—Edward Young, John Mills, William Brown, John Williams, Alexander Smith, Matthew Quintal, William McCoy and Isaac Martin—into battle with the Tubaians, in the hope of colonising Tubai and beginning a new life, but the venture failed. The party discovered Rarotonga, and finally settled on Pitcairn Island in 1790. In the first year of settlement, Christian put down a revolt of the native men, and the subsequent peace was uneasy. He took a Tahitian wife, Maimiti, whom he called Isabella, and the couple had two sons, Thursday October and Charles, and a daughter, Mary Ann Christian, who was born on the day of Christian's death.

Christian's end came in 1793. Ironically, he was killed in an uprising triggered by the outrage of four Polynesian men—Teimua, Niau, Minarii and Tetahiti—at the treatment they had

Bounty Bay in Pitcairn Island, where Christian and his supporters settled in 1790, after the mutiny received from the English settlers, whereby the men were denied women companions because the settlers took the local women as wives. As he worked in his garden, Christian was shot and clubbed to death. Rumours remain in circulation suggesting that Christian escaped from Pitcairn and returned to England. Glynn Christian asserts that he investigated each of the 11 conflicting stories of the mutineer's death and found no evidence that any had credibility other than the brutal tale of Christian's 'broken head blackening in the red soil of Pitcairn'.

Too often, Christian's actions are defined solely in terms of the mutiny against Bligh and the ill-fated voyage of the *Bounty*. His deeds viewed through this lens are certainly rash and are those of a pirate and blackbirder. Christian was also a significant and little-acknowledged explorer and navigator. He was the founding father of a unique group of people on Pitcairn—a new society, founded through necessity. True to his family's lineage as administrators of justice, Christian ensured that Pitcairn was the first community to give full franchise to women.

James Morrison

James Morrison is the only one of the 25 mutineers about whom we know more than the scanty physical description noted down by Bligh. His diary survived as a chronicle of the voyage and the personalities of those on the *Bounty*. Aged 28 at the time of the mutiny, Morrison was 5 feet 8 inches tall with a sallow complexion, long black hair and of slender build. His duties as gunner on previous assignments had resulted in the loss of the use of his forefinger's upper joint on his right hand. A star was tattooed on his left breast and around a garter shape on his left leg was tattooed the motto 'honi soit qui mal y pense' (evil be to him who evil thinks). A musket ball had badly scarred one arm.

Morrison was an educated man who joined the navy at 17 as a midshipman and became a qualified master gunner. He had also passed an examination in elementary navigation. It is quite possible that he sought a position in the scientific and explorative expedition because of the possibility of opportunities arising in any venture touching the West Indies and its trade potential. He missed appointment as gunner, but was signed on regardless as boatswain's mate. His writing is intelligent, experienced and exhibits a detachment with which he made fair judgments of Bligh's behaviour. In his opinion, Bligh's loyalist officers could have quelled the mutiny if they had tried.

Like Christian, Morrison revealed a contradictory personality suggesting a man who was grappling with the conflicting currents of social change which pushed and pulled at his progress through life. Morrison outspokenly criticised the Establishment and yet was tattooed with the star from the conservative decoration, Most Noble Order of the Garter. Onboard his several ship appointments he was known as a strong advocate for his rights and those of his fellow crew members. At the time of the mutiny, he acted as boatswain for the mutineers, but the detached way in which he expressed himself in his diary gives him an air of a man acting as a facilitator rather than a committed rebel.

After the mutiny, Morrison chose to live on Tahiti with his close friend, Poeno, a chief of the Matavai district. In time, he became advisor to Chief Matte and he might have eventually become king and sovereign of all Tahiti. While his political involvement deepened, Morrison designed and built a 30-ton schooner in which he intended to sail to Batavia (now Jakarta) in the Dutch East Indies and then on to England. He did not divulge his plans to those who helped him build the vessel, telling them it was for excursions in local waters. In fact, this was exactly the purpose it fulfilled, as there was no proper canvas and rope for sails, no navigation equipment and no storage vessels for water or food.

Morrison did eventually return to England, where he was tried and found guilty but received the highest recommendation of mercy. Returning to active duty as a warrant officer, he served through the great naval battles of St Vincent, the Nile, Copenhagen and Trafalgar. On 1 February 1807, Morrison went down with the old ship, the *Blenheim*, in a ferocious gale off the coast of Madagascar. This was the vessel on which he had trained as a young gunner before signing on to the *Bounty*. Despite his diarised criticisms of the British navy, he died doing his duty and serving the Crown.

A view in Matavai, Tahiti

'served 2 Gills of Grog'

The provisions

The Provisions were 150 lbs of Bread 16 pieces Pork 6 Quarts of Rum — 6 bottles of Wine 28 Galls of Water and 4 Empty Breakers — the Pork was in 2 lb pieces. —

We were very deep & rowed towards Tofoa — 25 Men remained on board with Christian. —

29 April

At dark got to the Island — could not land — served 2 Gills of Grog to each person. — In the morning landed with difficulty, in search of Provisions. — served a morsel of

28 April 1789 (continued)

The Provisions were 150 lbs of Bread 16 pieces Pork 6 Quarts of Rum—
6 bottles of Wine 28 Gallˢ of Water and 4 Empty Breakers—the Pork was in
2 lb pieces.—
We were very deep & rowed towards Tofoa—25 Men remained on board
with Christian.—

29 April 1789

At dark got to the Island—could not land—served 2 Gills of Grog
[=half a pint of diluted rum] to each person—
In the morning landed with difficulty, in search of Provisions—served a
Morsel of Bread & Jill [=gill] of Wine to each Person for Dinner.—

30 April 1789

Hard Gales.—At Night served a Cocoa Nut to each Man & slept again in the
Boat.—dared not venture to sea—At Dawn of Day served a Morsel of Bread &
a Spoonful of Rum to each Person landed in search of Provisions
At Noon wrote up all my transactions in my fair Book

1 May 1789

Had no success in Provisions at Night supped on a Plantain & a Gill of
Grog—At Dawn of Day sent Party away again

As Bligh waited to board the launch alongside the *Bounty*, argument raged on the vessel about what should be given to the company and what should remain. In Bligh's notebook, the list of provisions is brief—bread, pork, alcohol and water.

James Morrison's journal provides an account of the dispute between Chas Churchill, the master-at-arms, and William Purcell, the carpenter, about the latter's chest which Churchill wanted to keep on the *Bounty*, but which Christian ordered to be placed into the launch. Also loaded into the boat were masts and sails, new light canvas and nails, saws, the lieutenant's and master's clothes, as well as:

> two Gang Casks of Water, four empty breeves [small casks for water], 3 bags of Bread with Mr. Blighs Case, Some Bottles of Wine and several other things ... after Mr. Bligh was In the Boat he beggd for His Commission and Sextant; the Commission was Instantly Given him with his Pocket Book and private Journal by Mr. Christians order, and He took His own Sextant.

So weighed down was the boat that several items were thrown overboard. Bligh's plea for a musket was not granted, but four cutlasses were handed over, and Morrison, by his own account, passed the men in the launch about 25 four-pound pieces of pork (substantially more than the amount that Bligh had reported in his notebook) and two gourds of water.

Boobies were part of the men's diet, when they were fortunate enough to catch them

Christian had no wish to send the launch party away to a certain death. He expected that Bligh would make for the nearby Tongan Islands and wait there for an English ship. The launch had full provisions for 19 men for only five days, but this was more than enough to reach the islands. However, Bligh's landing on Tofua was ill-fated and he was forced to press on towards Timor with only a few coconuts and some damaged breadfruit to show for the shore visit.

It is at this point in the journey that most historians agree that it was Bligh's iron will and stubborn adherence to a relentless regime of rationing and navigational calculations that kept the craft on course and saved the lives of the men he sailed with. Both William Cole, the boatswain, and John Fryer, the master, were capable of navigating the course taken by Bligh, but we will never know if they would have possessed the discipline for the rigorous rationing needed to keep everyone alive.

Bligh's party faced an unpredictable voyage in the open boat

To get the launch to Timor, Bligh's original target was an ounce of bread and a quarter of a pint of water per day. He was able to raise the amount of water to a quarter of a pint three times a day, after the party was able to collect rainwater in a storm. Based on need, Bligh also gave his men a small portion of pork, coconut milk and an occasional teaspoonful of rum. He constructed a pair of scales made of coconut shells and used musket balls for weights so that he could weigh all rations fairly. As he approached the coast of New Holland, he calculated that he had enough food at the current ration rate for 29 more days. He omitted the supper ration to increase the food range to 43 days, as he was uncertain whether he could find Coupang (now Kupang, West Timor).

As the launch came closer to land, the number of birds flying near enough to catch by hand increased. The men caught boobies, tore them apart and distributed every part amongst themselves. Inside the reef, other food was available, such as oysters, tops of palm trees, fern roots and berries, compensating for the pork that had all been consumed. This supplementary food probably made the difference between surviving and perishing.

In the last stage of the voyage, as Bligh entered the Arafura Sea, rations were augmented with oysters and birds and, on 9 June, a dolphin was caught on a line attached to the boat. This was the first animal caught and landed despite the fact that the line had been out for the entire voyage. The means for sharing out this unexpected booty was a traditional sailor's method called 'Who shall have this?'. One man turned away while another pointed to the portions separately, asking aloud, 'Who shall have this?', to which the person with the averted gaze randomly called out a name. This means of allocating portions eliminated the risk of allegations about favouritism.

When the launch reached Coupang, food for 11 days remained, vindicating Bligh's careful rationing. Surplus or not, the survivors were a sorry sight as they were welcomed on dry land, having covered around 4000 miles, a staggering distance, in an open boat.

Bligh sighted Booby Island in the Torres Strait on 4 June 1789

'we eat under great apprehension of the Natives'
Tofua and indigenous relations

Saturday 2 May 1789

Stormy Wr. Wind ESE —

Natives came about us
endeavourd to [Cocoa Nutts] &
Plantains — could get no water
but 5 pints first trip 3 Gallons
afterwards — Natives became
hostile — at Noon served a
Cocoa Nutt & breadfruit to each
Kind for dinner which we
eat under great apprehension
of the Natives — copied in my Comd.

Sunday 3 May

[Fresh] Gales WW to NE
the Natives in great number
prepared to attack us — Ordered
all the People & what we had into
the Boat — then in, I followed &
the Natives began their attack
Killed Poor Norton — followed
us in Canoes — [Mauned] us
very much — [oared] out to Sea —

2 May 1789

Stormy W[r] Wind ESE—
Natives came about us endeavoured to [get?] Cocoa Nutts & Plantains—
could get no water but 5 pints first trip 3 Gallons afterwards—Natives
became hostile—at Noon served a Cocoa Nutt & Breadfruit to each Person
for dinner which we eat under great apprehension of the Natives—Copied in
my Jrnl.

3 May 1789

Fresh Gales ESE to NE
The Natives in great number prepared to attack us—I ordered all the People
& what we had into the Boat—When in, I followed & the Natives began
their attack Killed Poor Norton—followed us in Cannoes—maimed us very
much—rowed out to Sea—and after supplication from People at 8 at Night
bore away for Timor after prayers, agreeing to live on a Gill of Water &
morsel of Bread
our Stock of Provisions about 150 lbs Bread 28 gall[s] Water 20 lbs Pork
3 Bottles of Wine & 5 Quts Rum
The difference from our 1st quantity being owing to loss—a few Coconutts
& some Breadfruit were in the Boat but the latter useless.—divided into
2 watches & set a reefed lug foresail—at 8 am it blew a mere storm & were
in very eminant Danger—always bailing & in a horrible situation. served a
teaspoonful of Rum to each Person for we were very wet & Cold—
At Noon lat[d] 19[0] 27'S 183.52 E

Bligh and his party attempting to land on Tofua

When Bligh left the *Bounty* in the launch, he set course for Tofua, 30 miles away. Its location was marked by a smoke smudge on the skyline issuing from the island's active volcano. Christian had given Bligh his personal sextant, a compass, a quadrant, a timekeeper and tables for determining latitude and longitude. In his letters, Bligh did not refer to all his navigational equipment, possibly seeking to magnify the achievement of the journey he made to Timor by minimising the assistance he had on board.

On Tofua, Bligh hoped to replenish provisions before pressing on to Timor. He had no intention of adhering to the plan Christian had envisaged of waiting for an English vessel to appear to effect a rescue. Instead, he made for shore to prepare for the long voyage ahead. It was at this point that his ability to relate to the indigenous inhabitants of the island failed him. He made the mistake of telling them that he had been shipwrecked, thereby revealing their weakened circumstances. Commentators have pilloried Bligh for making this disclosure, but analysis of his orders given on Tahiti concerning the treatment of the South Sea Islanders confirms that he wanted all interaction with these people to be peaceful, respectful and non-threatening. Arms were not to be used.

Orders issued upon our Arrival at Otaheite, to regulate our Intercourse with the Natives.

Rules to be observed by every Person on Board, or belonging to the Bounty, for the better establishing a trade for Supplies of Provisions, and good Intercourse with the Natives of the South Sea, wherever the Ship may be at.

1st. At the Society, or Friendly Islands, no person whatever is to intimate that Captain Cook was killed by Indians; or that he is dead.

2d. No person is ever to speak, or give the least hint, that we have come on purpose to get the bread-fruit plant, until I have made my plan known to the chiefs.

3d. Every person is to study to gain the good will and esteem of the natives; to treat them with all kindness; and not to take from them, by violent means, any thing that they may have stolen; and no one is ever to fire, but in defence of his life.

4th. Every person employed on service, is to take care that no arms, or implements of any kind under their charge, are stolen; the value of such thing, being lost, shall be charged against their wages.

5th. No man is to embezzle, or offer to sale, directly, or indirectly, any part of the King's stores, of what nature soever.

6th. A proper person or persons will be appointed to regulate trade, and barter with the natives; and no officer or seaman, or other person belonging to the ship, is to trade for any kind of provisions, or curiosities; but if such officer or seaman wishes to purchase any particular thing, he is to apply to the provider to do it for him. By this means a regular market will be carried on, and all disputes, which otherwise may happen with the natives will be avoided. All boats are to have every thing handed out of them at sun-set.

Given under my hand, on board the Bounty,

Otaheite, 25th October, 1788.

WM. BLIGH

Once again the question arises: was Bligh ridiculously naive or profoundly idealistic in revealing his distressed state to the Tofuans? He had witnessed Cook's death and knew how capricious the goodwill of the islanders could be. Nevertheless, he seems to have wanted to behave humanely, even when he was at his most vulnerable after the mutiny.

After locating a cave in which the men could shelter, in the steep cliffs on the shoreline of Tofua, Bligh sent out provisioning parties, but these returned little in the way of food. A few coconuts were gathered and some damaged breadfruit, which Bligh described as 'useless'. As time went on, the local people gathered in increasing numbers, becoming more hostile. The launch party was clearly ill-equipped with weapons, four inadequate cutlasses being their only protection. On 2 May 1789, the attack came and, battling the rough surf, Bligh's men were scarcely able to reach the launch. The moorings remained fastened. With true

In Tahiti Bligh issued his crew with a set of rules to ensure peaceful interaction with the indigenous people

bravery, quartermaster John Norton leapt from the launch and ran up the beach to unfasten the line, dying in the attempt. Miraculously, the rest of the crew escaped by throwing overboard pieces of clothing, which the pursuers stopped to retrieve.

In the account of his voyage sent to Joseph Banks from Timor, Bligh describes the attack, the inclement weather, the loss of some provisions from the launch and the injuries sustained by the crew.

> *1st May—Party out as Yesterday and found out the residence of the Natives, who brought Supplies of Cocoa Nuts and Bread Fruit, besides shells of Water, all of which I bought for Buttons, which we cut of our Cloaths. They all left us at Sun Down. Wr. [weather] so windy could not proceed to Sea.*

> *2nd.—In the Morning Two Cheifs Eegyeefou, and the other Maccaaccabou, came down, also two Cannoes came in and another Cheif called Vageetee, and having enquired our Situation, and my determination to proceed to Paulehou their King. Eegyeefou agreed as soon as it moderated to go with me. This readiness gave me pleasure, but in*

On arrival in Tahiti, Bligh ordered that, when meeting the indigenous people, 'no officer or seaman ... is to trade for any kind of provisions, or curiosities'

a few hours I had as much uneasyness, The Natives began to be very troublesome and shewed signs of hostilities towards us, We however thought they would go off at Sun down as they had done before, and that then I could leave the place without any risk. but it proved to the contrary for three Cannoes were now come in, and places were fixed on for their residence during the night, and fires made.

I therefore determined to do our best while it was light and directed some provisions we had Bought to be put into the Boat. The Cheifs desired I would Stay notwithstanding they perceived that I saw all their people were Arming with Clubs & Stones. We were now all on the go, and taking One of the Cheifs by the Hand, with a Cutlass in the

other, and my people with Sticks. we proceeded down to the Boat. when we were attacked by a Multitude of Indians in the course of which I lost a very worthy good man and the rest of us more or less bruized and Wounded.

This incident greatly altered Bligh's plans, as he explained in a letter to his wife's uncle, Duncan Campbell. He had at last realised that respect for their party was contingent on the use of firearms, and he possessed none:

I had determined to go to Amsterdam in search of Paulehow the King, but taking this as a Sample of their Natural dispositions there were little hopes to expect much from them, for I considered their good behaviour hitherto owing to a dread of our Fire Arms, which now knowing us to have none would not be the Case, & that supposing our lives were in safety—Our Boat and every thing would be taken from us and thereby I should never be able to return. I was also earnestly sollicited by all hands to take them towards home, and when I told them no hopes of releif for us remained, but what I might find at New Holland. untill I came to Timor, a distance of 1200 leagues or more, they all agreed to live on one ounce of bread pr. day and a Jill of Water. I therefore after recommending this as a sacred promise forever to their Memory, bore away for New Holland and Timor across a Sea but little known and in a small Boat deep loaded with 18 Souls, without a Single Map of any kind, and nothing but my own recollection and general knowledge of the Situation of Places to direct us.

On 3 May 1789, Timor was a very long way off. Badly bruised, shocked at the attack and the death of the crew's comrade, and dreading the thought of the endurance test that lay ahead, Bligh prepared mentally for what would become the most famous open-boat voyage in maritime history.

'Our three Watches'
The Bounty launch

Monday 4 May Cont.

saw land a smell hill and heights
It was now Noon great difficulty
I could obsrve the Sun alt.
Let'd in 10.° 50' S 182.16 E — divided
5 small Coco Nutts for our Dinner
every one was satisfied. —

our three watches to be

Mr. Fryer	Mr. Cole	Mr. Peckover
Purcel	Elphinston	Hayward
Simpson	Lebogue	Linkletter
Tinkler	Hallet	Samuels
Ledward	Nelson	Hall
Mr. Lamb		Mr. Smith

4 May 1789

D⁰ W𝗿 & distresses great & in the greatest danger of foundering Served a
teaspoon full of Rum

Saw land a small Isl𝖽 mod height It was now Noon great difficulty I could
observe the Suns Alt𝖽 Lat𝖽 in 18° 58'S 182.16 E—Divided 5 Small Coco Nutts
for our Dinners Every one was satisfied.—
Our three Watches to be

M𝗋 Fryer	M𝗋 Cole	M𝗋 Peckover
Purcel	Elphinston	Hayward
Simpson	Lebogue	Linkletter
Tinkler	Hallet	Samuels
Ledward	Nelson	Hall
Jn Lamb		Jn⁰ Smith

[Some calculations omitted here]

Disc𝖽 a small Flat Isl𝖽 of a small height at Noon WSW 4 or 5 leag𝗌

Dimensions

	Ft.	ins.
Length	23	0
Breadth	6	9
Depth	2	9

		Ft.	ins.
Stem sided		0	3½
Keel Do. Midships		0	3⅞
Post sided at the	Tuck	0	3½
	Alow	0	3
Transom thick		0	2
Floor Timbers	Sided	0	2
	Moulded at the Heads	0	2⅛
	Throat	0	3⅞
Futtocks	Sided Alow	0	2
	Square at the Heads	0	1⅞

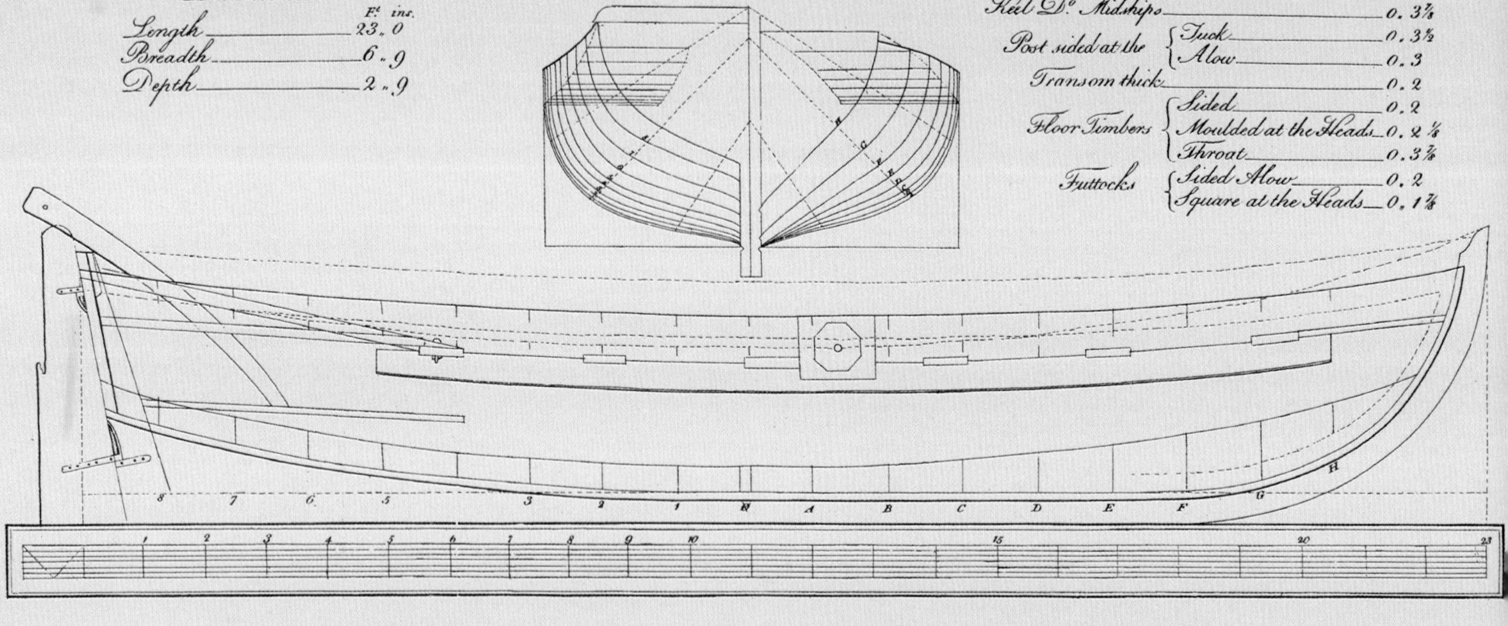

A Copy of the Draught from which the Bounty's Launch was built.

Mackenzie

W hen the *Bounty* was being fitted out for the Pacific expedition, the original complement of boats was to include a launch of 20-feet length, a cutter of 18 feet and a jolly boat of 16 feet. However, the deadline precluded the Deptford yard meeting these requirements and, after another incident in which a second contractor's boats were damaged, the launch that was finally supplied was built in the Isle of Wight, taken across to Portsmouth and placed onboard the *Bounty*. Documents relating to the manufacture of the launch were discovered 140 years later in the offices of the maker, John Samuel White of Cowes. In the 1930s, author and boat designer Uffa Fox found fragments of a letter in White's offices from Bligh thanking White for building such a robust vessel, together with a copy of the draughts for the launch. The letter is thought to have been destroyed subsequently after a new firm bought out the company.

Debate about the launch's construction continues. Stephen Walters, in his edition of Fryer's account of its journey, maintains that the launch was built using the double-diagonal construction style, a technique invented by Thomas White, the founder of the shipbuilding company. The method uses two thicknesses of the outer skin planking worked flush-edged, the skins being worked 45 degrees to the keel in opposite directions to each other. The inner layer has the gunwale ends running aft, producing a very strong vessel. Jasper Shackleton, who built a replica of the launch to retrace Bligh's journey in 1989, commented that although White built many double-diagonal hulls, this technique was not used until after the *Bounty* had left England. In the construction of his vessel, Shackleton opted for a compromise, using carvel construction for the planking underneath and clinker on the top sides.

The *Bounty* launch was 23 feet in length with a breadth of 6 feet 9 inches. She had a gentle curvature, allowing her to sit well in the water. Probably built of larch planking, she was balanced by the weight of the windlass, which was used for heaving heavy cables over the

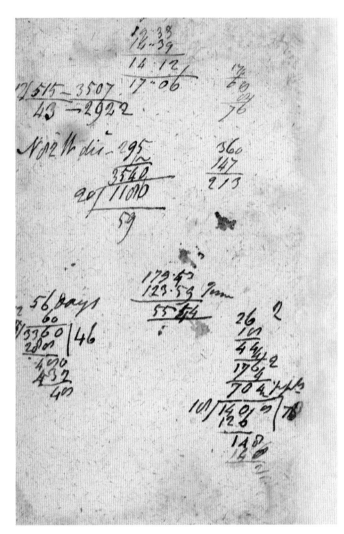

An undated page of calculations at the beginning of the notebook showing Bligh's early efforts at determining the course, the distance and the time it would take to get to Timor

A copy of the draught from which the *Bounty*'s launch was built

Don McIntyre in the boat in which he and three others, in 2010, replicated Bligh's journey in the launch (the boat does not reflect the size or exact design of the *Bounty* launch)

fairlead within the derrick on its stern. This apparatus was used to tow the mother ship or to do maintenance work on her anchors or cables. The windlass also kept the sides of the launch evenly apart and took the strain from oncoming waves. With one mast, she probably also had a lug sail and her displacement is thought to have been 5.57 tons.

Modern mariners have marvelled at how Bligh managed the lack of space with a crew who were in poor physical and mental health. Bligh wrote that the launch was only big enough for half the occupants to rest at a time. It was certainly his ability to take charge of food rationing, maintain morale and make sure the launch was not swamped that represents Bligh's finest achievement. His navigational feats were laudable, but could probably have been replicated by several others in the launch. It was his indefatigable determination to follow standard naval procedures and routines calmly and accurately in appalling conditions that helped keep sanity and order amongst the demoralised crew, enabling the launch to reach Timor safely.

Bligh's methods involved simple rhumb-line sailing and he made plane and mid-latitude calculations with traverse tables. The information that he required to make these calculations was derived from a Ramsden 10" sextant, a quadrant, an Adam's compass from the *Bounty*'s binnacle and a logline, fabricated in the launch in the early days of the voyage to teach the men how to calculate speed and thence plot the vessel's progress more accurately.

How must the seamen have felt when, having reached safety in the East Indies in this noble craft, they were forced to sell it in order to subsidise the purchase and fitting out of the *Resource*, in which Bligh transported his men to Batavia:

> *As no one could be hired but at a Price equal to a Purchase, I therefore gave publick Notice of my Intent and assisted by the governor I got a vessel for 1000 Rix Dollars and called her the* Resource.

Bligh documented his frustration at the delay in communication caused by slow seamail. It must have felt strange to Bligh to have passed through such an ordeal on a craft like the *Bounty* launch and still be far removed from the people to whom news of his safety was so important. Both the Admiralty and Bligh's family would remain in ignorance of his amazing feat for some months after the adventure had been concluded. Until he arrived home in England in March 1790, Bligh would have ample time to reflect on the series of circumstances that had placed him in the unenviable position of being a commander who had lost his ship:

> *There is but little Chance that their Lordships can receive this before I arrive myself I therefore have not been as particular as I shall be in my Letter from Batavia. I shall sail in the Morning without fail, and use my utmost Exertions to appear before their Lordships and answer personally for the Loss of His Majesty's Ship.*

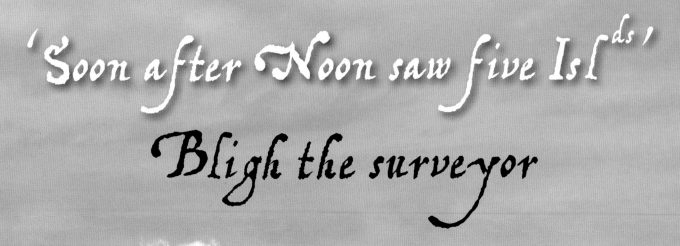

'Soon after Noon saw five Isl^{ds}'
Bligh the surveyor

5th May Tuesd.y 1 PM noon After
Noon saw five Isl.d comp.g the first seen
to the WSW — A large Isl.d to NW & one
to the W½SW —

At 10 after 3 saw an other Isl.d making
in all 6 — south Isl.d bore south. The
North Isl.d NWbN, next NWbW½sW; the
next WbN, next SbW, next SbW
next SbW, next SbW a rock close to the
south Isl.d —

NbW¾W¾S 8
6 chagues

At 4.h 34.' North Isl.d Were North 5 or 6 leag.s

NWbW¾W 18 — 9,3 — 15,4 — 17,
18
25
10.50
10.33

102.16
101.59 E. North Isl.d

Soon after Noon saw five Isl^ds count^g the first seen to the WSW—A large Isl^d to NW & one to the WNW—
At 10 after 3 an other Isl^d making in all 8—South Isl^d bore South. The North Isl^d NWbN, next NWbW½W, the next WSW, next SSW, next SbW
next S½W, next S[?] a Rock close to the South Isl^d—

NWbW¼W18—9:3—15.4=17

$$\begin{array}{ll} 16 & 182.16 \\ \hline 25 & 181.59E:North\ Isl^d \end{array}$$

[Sketch map of the Windward Islands of Fiji omitted here]

At 4°.34' North Isl^d true North 5 or 6 leag

Signals for Boats
Sent to Discover Anchorage
On Finding bottom to be denoted in the following Manner
1st. : 5 fathoms a blue flag.
2^d. : 10 fathoms a White flag.
3^d. : 15 fathoms a Red flag.
4th. : 20 fathoms a White and Red flag both held up Together
5th. : For every fathom between 5 and 10—10 and 15—15 and 20 fathoms the flag to be lowered and held up, first making the particular signal distinctly; holding it up one Minute, and the repeaters a Quarter of a Minute between Each.
6th. : 30 fathoms and upwards a White, and a Blue flag and for every fathom up to 40, the White flag to be lower'd and held up.
7th. : A good harbour or safe Anchorage the three flags to be hoisted together.
8th. :On discovering Danger, it is to be denoted by firing shotts, and that is to be Continued untill you
This was part of our Signel Book wch was in Mr Haywards Pocket & served me to make my occurrences in [this is written across the above in Bligh's hand as explanation]

At 5 PM saw two more Isl^ds to the Westward.—
They are all of a tolerable height and woody—The northernmost is the highest & has two small Isl^ds off its NE End—
At Sun Set North Is^ld NNE 5 leag^s & the West Isl^d in sight NW½W 8 leag^s—

[Some calculations omitted here]

D to Sunset
Marked a log line and taught the Men to count seconds

bel Tasman was the first European to discover the north-easternmost island of the Fijian archipelago, in February 1643; 131 years later, James Cook, on his second voyage in 1774, discovered a small island in the south-east of the group which he named Turtle Island. Bligh was the first European navigator to sail through the archipelago and chart its length. Between 5 and 8 May 1789, he navigated the launch through the middle of the islands from south-west to north-west, sighting the mountains of Viti Levu and departing through Round Island Passage. He returned to the archipelago on his second voyage in 1792, sailing from Mothe Island through the Koro Sea north until Taveuni came into view. He then turned south, sailing to the south-west extremity of Kandavu, and was able to connect this exploration with his earlier discoveries.

In the short account of the launch's voyage, which he included in a letter he wrote from Batavia to Joseph Banks in October 1789, Bligh briefly describes the sighting of the Fijian Islands, his note about the weather serving as a reminder of the treacherous conditions in which the open launch continued its journey:

> *The Weather very boisterous and obliged to keep right before the Sea. which at times run into us and nearly filled the Boat, and were obliged to throw all spare Cloaths overboard, and every Article we could possibly do without.*
>
> *On the 4th. May Latitude 18°:50' So Longd. 182°:16 Et I discover'd Land an Island. WSW. 4 or 5 Leagues. On the 6th. Discovered Ten other Islands, and that day at noon was in Latd. 17°:53 So. & Longd. 179:43 East. Many Shoals. On the 7th. discovered other Islands, At Noon Latitude 16°:33' So. 178°:34 Et. were chased by Two large Cannoes but got clear of them by Rowing. At Night torrents of Rain with Thunder & Lightning, Caught 6 Gallons Water.*

After the loss of Norton on Tofua, Bligh could not countenance visiting inhabited islands again. The lack of firearms made the crew vulnerable to attack. It must have been agonising to navigate through the Fijian archipelago, glimpsing the lush vegetation, streams and waterfalls carrying fresh water and not to go ashore.

The frontispiece from a 1790 Dutch translation of Bligh's *Narrative of the Mutiny on Board His Majesty's Ship* Bounty

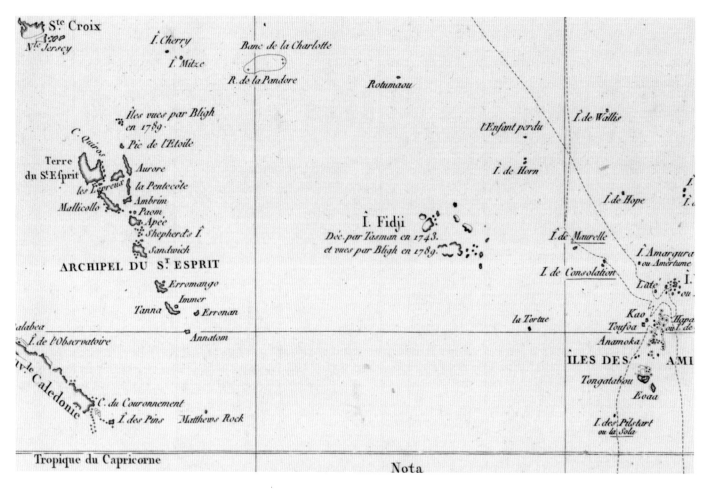

A detail of a 1797 map, showing the Fijian archipelago, through which Bligh navigated in early May 1789

In the remarks Bligh entered in the log for 5 May, he expanded on the hasty maps and calculations made in the notebook, adding details about how he imagined the islands to be fertile. His description of the meal in the launch makes a melancholy comparison with the verdant islands they could not risk investigating:

> I now fixed on Steering WNW for the night and stood on under a Reefed Foresail. Served a few broken peices of Breadfruit for Supper and performed prayers. The night turned out fair and Smooth water and having had tolerable Rest, our Spirits and Strength by the morning seemed vastly better and we very contentedly breakfasted on a few peices of yams that were found in the Boat. After breakfast we prepared a Chest for our Bread and got it secured by noon, but unhappily a great deal was damaged and Rotten. This nevertheless we were obliged to keep for use.

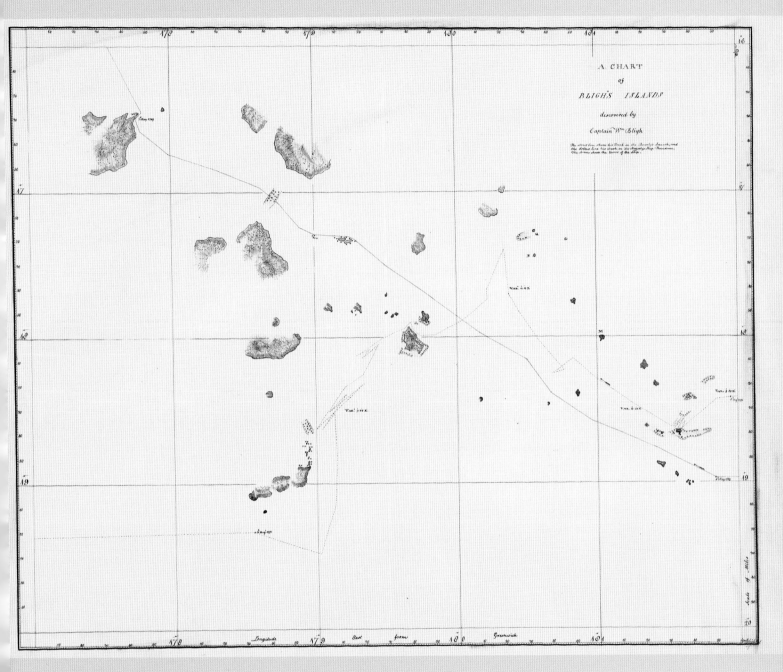

Bligh's chart of Bligh's Islands, the name he gave the Fijian Islands while on his 1792 voyage in the *Providence*

A view of the Fijian Islands—Bligh would not land here for fear of attack by the indigenous inhabitants

A harbour in Fiji in the 1850s—passing through the islands of 'Fidgee', Bligh's launch was chased by local inhabitants in two large canoes; it was only around 50 years later, when this image was painted, that sandalwood traders and missionaries began to live among the Fijians

Bligh refers to his strategy of getting the crew involved in the navigation:

> *I have hitherto been only able to keep an imperfect account of our Run, but have now got ourselves a little better equipped and a line marked, & having practiced counting seconds, every one can do it with some exactness.*

His account of sighting Fiji provides just a hint of the curiosity he probably felt and shows an attempt to give the best description possible of the islands despite his constraints. Also evident is the active voice which he uses in both his notebook and his logbook, never admitting that his writing might never reach another living being should the boat capsize. He was determined to leave a navigational legacy of the region for those who followed, writing in his logbook:

> *The Land I have passed is very likely to be a part of those Islands called Fidgee. They lie between the latitude of 19°05'So. & 18°19'So and between the longitude of 182°02' and 181°33'Et. The largest may be about 6 leagues in Circuit but it is impossible for me to be very exact. To show where they are to be found again is doing a great deal in my present situation. The sketch I have made of them will give a better Idea of their situation and Extent. I believe all the larger Isles are inhabited as they appeared very fertile.*

'Land to lew^d from
WNW to WSW'

Bligh's navigational skills

H	K	F	Courses	Winds	Thursd. 7th May 1789
1	3		NWbN	ENE	mod. fair
2	3				
3	3		"	"	saw another Isld to the NNW
4	3		WNW	"	
5	3	3		"	The above Isld we found join
6	1	6	WbS	"	to the one set at Noon NbWbW
7	3	6	served a ½ill of		Pbt 5¼. The extrems of the above
8	4	4	water & a bit		Island from NbW½W to NE½E
9	4	2	of bread —		land as far as SWbW on the
10	4	2			So & NW½W on the north paid
11	4				over a reef wt 4 feet water
12	4	4			
1	4				light squalls
2	3	4			to leward
3	3	3			At day discovered land &
4	3				from WbNW to WbSW like
5	4				numbers of high Rocky Islds
6	3			NE	& some low land from 8 to 4
7	3		NNW		Leag: dist. A high round
8	3		NWbN	SEbNt	Hill SEt N NW 6 leag. &
9	2¼		NW	NbE	land SSE the same as set
10	1		WNW		SWbW last night
10	1		NNW	NE	at 9h ½ h. Extrem Land to leu.
11	2	4			NW 5 leag. to SWbW½NW a high
12	2	4		"	Rock 5 leag. — High Islds NEbE
					Cloudy & hazie Wr Curri set to

no towds the shore two in all Isles WbNW 2 Mile
being the North extreme of the land — saw two
within Cannoes coming to us — Out oars to
get from them. Southern. Land SbW

7 *May* 1789 _____

H	K	F	Courses	Winds	Thursd^y 7th May 1789

[H = hour of day; K = knots; F = fathoms]

H	K	F	Courses	Winds	
1	3		NWbN	ENE	Mod. & fair
2	3				
3	3		"	"	Saw another Isl^d to the NNW
4	3		WNW	"	
5	3	3		"	the above Isl^d we found join to the one set at Noon NbW1/2W
6	1	5	WbN		
2	2				At 5¾—The extrem^s of the above Island from NbW½W to NE½E
7	3	6	Served a Jill of water & a bit of bread—		
8	4	4			
9	4	2			Land as far as SWbW on the S^o & NW½W on the north pas^d over a reef wth 4 feet water
10	4	2			
11	4				
12	4	4			
1	4				light squalls
2	3	4			
3	3	3			At day discovered land to leward from WNW to WSW like numbers of high Rocky Isl^ds & some low land from 8 to 4 leag^s dis^t—A high round Hill Isl^d NNW 6 leag^s & land SSE the same as set SWbW last night
4	3				
5	4				
6	3			NE	
7	3		NNW	—	
8	3		NWbN	NEbN	
9	2	¼	NW	NNE	
10	1		WNW		
1			NNW	NE	At 9½[E?] Extrem^s Land to lew^d NW 5 leag^s to SWbW½W a high Rock 5 leag.—High Isl^d NbE
11	2	4			
12	2	4			Cloudy & Varie W^r Curr. sets us

towd^s the Shore two small Isls WNW 2 Miles being the north extreme of
the land—Saw two sailing cannoes coming to us—
Out oars to get from them Souther^n Land SbW

Thursd. 7th May   N   W
N N W g miles 8,9 - 3,9   14   1. 9
A W b W S ——— 5,0 7,5   1.33   170.34

N N W 49 ——— 10,0 25,3   Course N 56 W 79 W

N W b N 2/4 W 9 — 7.0 - 5,0
N 10 b W — 6 — 5,0, 3, 3
44,1 65,1

Frid. 8th   Lat 47 - 16: 33 — 578: 3/56
                 Obs — 16 - 4   5 56

N W b W 17 - 14,1 - 91,4   29   177.3 09

N W b W 60 46,9 - 33

64·0· 42   Course N 62 W
45   Dis. 62
0 09   Diff 54 = 56
54

9th. W N W 66 61,0 - 25,0 Lat 47 - 16· 04 — 177: 30
.11.30 — 157·55   Obs — 15: 47   1· 3

One of the interesting discrepancies between Bligh's account of his voyage and the evidence provided by the other crew members who had kept written records of the mutiny is the matter of navigational equipment. Bligh was at great pains to state that, in the launch, he had only an old compass, an old quadrant and an old book of positions. In fact, Morrison's and Fryer's accounts of the departure from the *Bounty* indicate that Christian and his men had provided Bligh with all the necessary items to calculate a course and make a sea journey in relative safety. Bligh's main technical disadvantage was the inability to determine longitude correctly, as he had no proper timekeeper and no nautical almanac with which he could have resorted to the lunar method of calculating longitude. While he lamented his lack of navigational instruments, Bligh was equipped with the navigational tools that every mariner would have had to make do with up until 20 years before his voyage—and he had endurance.

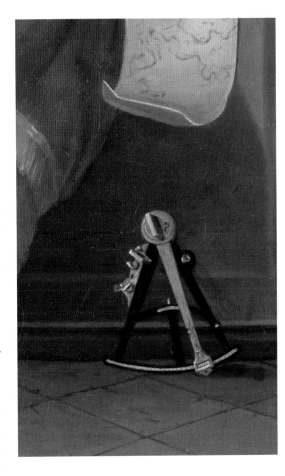

A sextant of the early 1780s—a sextant had been among the navigational equipment that Christian had handed Bligh in the launch

It is, however, important to emphasise that Bligh carried out his calculations in extreme conditions. The boat was dangerously low in the water because of its 18 passengers (19 before the death of Norton), their provisions and equipment. The crew was also in a desperate state of physical discomfort, suffering from exposure and the effects of near malnutrition. All onboard the launch endured the constant fear of capsizing, pursuit and attack by hostile indigenous inhabitants, the threat of starvation and the dread of a navigational mistake that would seal their doom. It is Bligh's iron will and his implementation of a rigorous daily routine, coupled with his magnificent practical skill as a seaman, that is documented in the notebook. The calculations and the daily schedule, recorded in Bligh's hasty jottings, recreates a detailed pen-portrait of Bligh the great sailor—from the inside. Whenever the men left the launch on the rare occasions when the company reached land, conflict broke out but, at sea, Bligh was unquestionably master of his crew. At the most fundamental level, the crew trusted him as an excellent navigator.

What was the method Bligh used to navigate the course that brought the launch to safety? The term 'plane sailing', often corrupted to 'plain sailing', is used commonly in modern-day

A page of calculations from Bligh's notebook—on 7 May, cloudy weather meant that Bligh was unable to take the noon observation

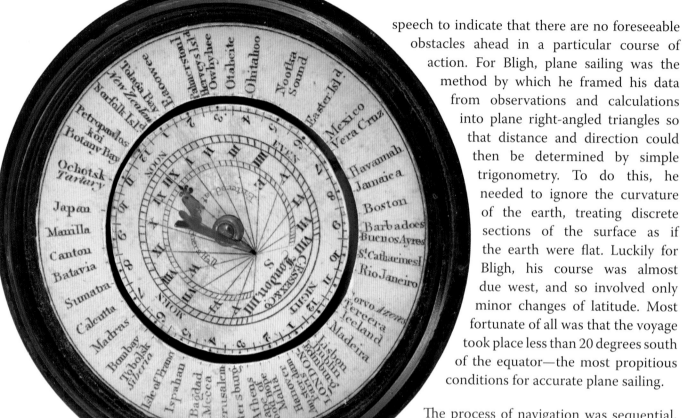

A compass, c.1780—Bligh emphasised the fragility of his circumstances by complaining that the only navigational tools he had on the launch were a compass, a quadrant and a book of positions

speech to indicate that there are no foreseeable obstacles ahead in a particular course of action. For Bligh, plane sailing was the method by which he framed his data from observations and calculations into plane right-angled triangles so that distance and direction could then be determined by simple trigonometry. To do this, he needed to ignore the curvature of the earth, treating discrete sections of the surface as if the earth were flat. Luckily for Bligh, his course was almost due west, and so involved only minor changes of latitude. Most fortunate of all was that the voyage took place less than 20 degrees south of the equator—the most propitious conditions for accurate plane sailing.

The process of navigation was sequential, relying on cumulative equations. Typical calculations for the day would begin at noon, derived from a position described in terms of south latitude and east longitude, based on calculations from the previous day. For the next 24 hours, the courses could be steered accurately using the *Bounty* compass. It was essential for the men in the launch to measure the distance run on each course by obtaining the launch's speed every hour which, when applied to the time taken for each course, gave the distance covered. This process necessitated the manufacture of a log—a quadrant-shaped piece of wood, weighted on the rim to stand upright in the water, to which a line knotted at regular intervals was attached. When the line was tossed over the stern, it would remain stationery while the launch sailed away from it, with the attached line running out freely. The speed in nautical miles an hour, knots, could be calculated immediately by counting the number of knots that went past within a specified time. It has been proposed that Bligh's line had a knot every 25 feet.

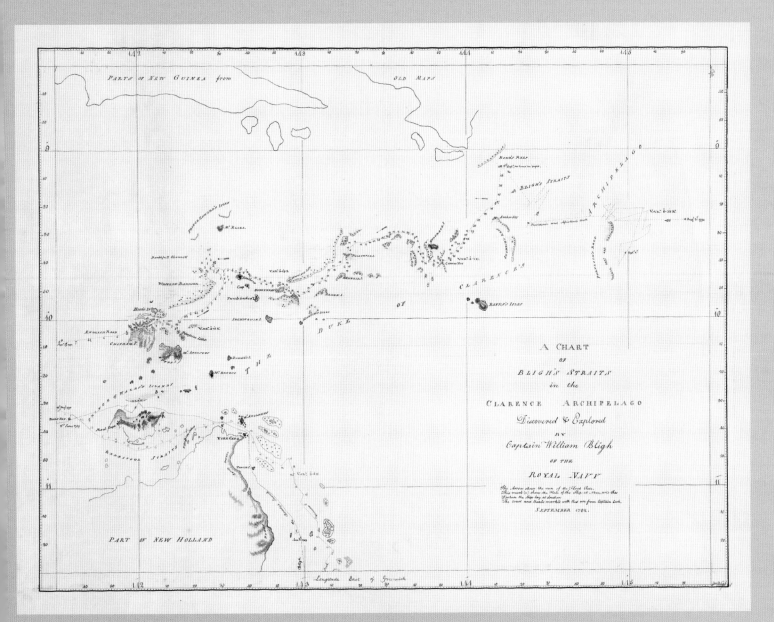

Bligh's chart of the islands in the Torres Strait, which he named the Clarence Archipelago in 1792

88

An eighteenth-century pocket watch—Bligh used a pocket watch as a timekeeper to determine longitude until 2 June, when the watch stopped working

Relatively simple trigonometry was the secret to Bligh's navigational success, verified by the set of traverse tables Bligh had in his possession. The tables calculated all right-angled triangles with a hypotenuse of up to 300 miles and enabled a navigator to get the correct answer to his equation by locating the relevant columns and following standard rules. At the end of the 24-hour period, all the courses sailed and distance run were resolved into right-angled triangles: the distance was the hypotenuse, the 'northing' or 'southing' in nautical miles was the vertical side, equal to the change of latitude in minutes of arc; and the distance in miles, made good towards the west, called 'departure', became the horizontal side of the triangle. By adding the vertical and horizontal distances, totals for each direction covered for that day were calculated. If it was impossible to see the sun at noon, the dead-reckoning position for that time was calculated by applying the change of latitude, or distance covered to the north or south, to the latitude of the previous day and subtracting the difference of longitude, calculated from the departure, from the previous longitude. As the meridians approach the poles they converge and the actual distance between them decreases predictably, in proportion to the cosine of the particular latitude. Bligh knew the departure and the mean average latitude of the day's sailing and readily calculated the difference of longitude.

The task requiring greatest focus in a small, cramped, tossing boat was the observation of the sun's altitude, and this Bligh managed to do unfailingly, enabling the launch to hold the course that would bring it to its destination. For greatest accuracy, Bligh needed to consistently observe the altitude of the sun with the sextant at noon each day. He would subtract the sun's declination, meaning the distance of the sun north or south of the equator, and keep a record of this in one of his books. By subtracting this altitude from 90 degrees, Bligh was able to find his actual latitude, within two nautical miles. To calculate actual latitude and a dead-reckoning longitude for the noon position that he had entered in his log, Bligh used the latitude midway between his observed latitude and that of the previous day, converting the departure into minutes of longitude.

Bligh stressed that he had only his memories of Cook's charts of the region to rely upon for information about the places lying to the west of Tofua, and an obsolete book of latitudes and longitudes. However, the calculations in the notebook of his course to Cape York and Timor suggest that he had found these figures in some other book he had with him in the vessel. His course has been described as following a time-honoured nautical trick of 'running down a parallel of latitude', which must eventually have led Bligh to the coast of New Holland, hitting the coast at a known point, as the line of the coast is almost precisely at right angles to his course. The variability of his calculations was demonstrated by the fact that the launch reached the expected landfall on the Great Barrier Reef nearly a day early.

One of the challenges for Bligh was his reliance for timekeeping on a pocket watch that he had borrowed from William Peckover, the *Bounty*'s gunner, with which to determine longitude. The watch kept working until 2 June, when it stopped and, from that point on, Bligh could only be sure of the times for sunrise, sunset and noon, but he managed to interpose the missing refinements by making a visual estimate of the sun's changing position to keep the 24-hour divisions in the log.

Understanding the structure of Bligh's notebook relies on adjusting from civil time to nautical time. Day in nautical terms starts at noon when the sun crosses the meridian, and this puts the first 12 hours of the nautical day one day ahead of the civil day. At midnight, halfway through the nautical day, the date coincides with that of the civil day, newly begun, lasting until noon.

Bligh's notebook is the record of a man hard at work with no time or inclination for lengthy philosophising. The author remained present in the moment and locked in concentration on the tasks at hand: unceasingly calculating navigational data, re-assessing food rationing, providing new strategies to keep the men warm and protected as much as possible from exposure, and always on the lookout for means of catching rainwater or snaring any passing animal or bird for food. In a superficial reading of the notebook, Bligh appears to function as an automaton, constantly calculating the mechanical processes for survival. However, the conventions of log writing and the physical restrictions which resulted in Bligh's terse, yet detailed, record offers food for the imagination. With a little willingness, we can look through the eyes of one of the eighteenth century's greatest seamen to appreciate the continuous threads of equations and observations with which Bligh wove the lifeline for the crew of the *Bounty* launch.

'At 6ʰ Saw land'
The influence of Joseph Banks

Thursd. 11th May 1786

1	4		W	SbW	Fresh Breezes & Cloudy
2	4		WbS		Got our Cloaths to lin to
3	6				dry — that things that
4	4				saved when wet
5	4				
6	4				Bread & Water for Supper
7	4				
8	4				
9	4				
10	6				
11	4				
12	3	6	West	SbW	at 6ᵇ saw land from
1	4				SWbS ½ that to NWbW ½
2	4	1			W 5 leag'. — Three rem
3	3	6			Hills the Northermost
4	3	6			the smallest & most
5	3	4			conical. WbN ¾ S WbS ½ S
6	4	4	NWbN		& W ¾ S 4 leag'. — High
7	4	4		SE	land & Inlets.
8	4	4			Very cloudy Mod Breezes
9	4	4	NWbW		The extr of the land
10	4	4			W ½ N. to SW ½ S 4 leag.
11	4	4			the S extreme being the
12	5		WbW		conical Hill (J. aberdie)

At Noon conical Hill & north W extreme
SbE 4 leag Large Inl. SW & WbW land
7 leag Small Inl MObN 4 leag

[H	K	F	Courses	Wind]	Thursd^y 14 May 1789
1		W		SbW	Fresh Breezes & Cloudy
2	4				
3	4	—	WbS	S^o	Got our Cloaths tolerably dry—what
4	4				things I had Saved rotten wth wet
5	4				
6	4	"	"	"	Bread & Water for Supp—
7	4				
8	4				
9	4				
10	4				
11	4				
12	4				
1	3	6	West	SbW	At 6^h Saw land from SWbS 7 leag^s
2	4				to NWbW¾ W 5 leag^s—Three
3	4	1			rem^r [remarkable?] Hills the
4	3	6			Northermost the smallest & most
5	3	6			Conical—WbS¾S WbS½S & W¾S
6	3	4			4 leag^s—High Land^s & Isl^ds—
7	4	4	NWbN		
8	4	4	"	SE	Very cloudy Mod^t Breezes
9	4	4	"	"	The extr^s of the land W½N. to
10	4	4	NWbW		SW½S 4 leag^s the S^o extreme being
11	4	4			the conical Hill (I. Averdi)
12	5	"	WNW		

South land set at first not in sight

At Noon, Conical Hill & north Ex^t as set before S½E 4 leag. large Isl^d
SSW½W & W. land West 7 leag^s A Small Isl^d NWbN 4 leag^s

[Sketch map of the Banks Islands omitted here]

On the East side of the West^n Isl^d appeared a fine Harbour, formed by the
whole Isl^d forms like a Crescent
The Points shut on at SbW & NbE
The land is High & slopes all round to the Bottom like a Bowl.—
The whole Country seems to be fertile and woody and Inhabited.

Cras Ingens iterabimus aequor.

*B*ligh's notebook entry for Thursday 14 May 1789 offers contrasting comments that reveal the continued deterioration of the crew's condition and the series of sightings that would have re-ignited Bligh's sense of purpose as expedition leader and helped to boost morale.

The first comment on matters other than the weather conditions records that clothing was now 'tolerably dry' but the description following reminds us of how dilapidated the men's attire had become and how extremely unpleasant it must have been to try and maintain some protection from the elements in garments that were 'rotten with wet'.

Bligh's next entry, 'Bread & Water for Supper', continues the theme of deprivation but, after six hours of not noting anything, Bligh records the sight of land, describing three hills, 'the Northernmost the smallest & most Conical'. Continually mindful of the debt he owed his patron, Joseph Banks, and keen to atone for the embarrassment of the mutiny by proving his worth as a surveyor, Bligh named the five islands the Banks Group (in the northern part of what is now known as Vanuatu). The mass of calculations and the sketch map of the islands illustrate the method and the art of the surveyor/cartographer, and the page would have provided satisfaction to Bligh as a palpable result of the day's painstaking work. He describes the West Island briefly, but almost affectionately, noting a 'fine Harbour' on the east side, and depicting the shape of the island as a 'bowl' with 'fertile and woody' vegetation. How tantalising the shore must have appeared to the ravenous men in the launch.

The islands were named as follows: Large Island (now Vanua Levu), West Island (Ureparapara), East Island (Mota Levu), North Rocks (Mota) and the unnamed island is now Gaua. Historians believe that this was not a new sighting and that the Spanish explorer, de Quiros, had discovered the group of islands in 1606. In the notebook, Bligh miscalculated and identified the conical hill as Pico de Averdi, which Cook had recorded on his 1777 *A Chart of the Southern Hemisphere Showing the Tracks of Some of the Most Distinguished Navigators*, based on voyages he made in the *Resolution* and the *Adventure* between 1772 and 1775. (In fact, Cook's Pico de Averdi is Pic de l'Etoile, Bouganville.) When preparing for the voyage on the *Bounty*, Bligh would have studied Cook's work to familiarise himself with useful landmarks and to gain an understanding of the Pacific region.

In naming the islands after Banks, Bligh was recording his devotion to the patron who had secured his appointment as commander of the *Bounty*. He was also commemorating Banks' role in both the exploration of the Pacific region and in the investigation and documentation of many aspects of natural history and cultural practices on his voyage with Cook on the

Joseph Banks, 1774

Endeavour. Banks was the son of a wealthy Lincolnshire squire and a Fellow of the Royal Society, living on an inheritance of £6000 per annum. He had attended Oxford University, but had never graduated, consolidating his botanical knowledge as a kind of apprentice to Dr Daniel Solander, a student of Carl Linnaeus and one of the foremost botanists of the time. The apprenticeship involved Banks paying Solander £400 to accompany him on the *Endeavour* expedition, a reverse in the usual order of the relationship between master and learner. Banks contributed £10 000 to Cook's voyage. He travelled with a retinue of seven, claiming the captain's berth as his own and using the great cabin as his work space. Solander was Banks' assistant, along with naturalist Herman Spöring, a professor of medicine, an astronomer and two artists. By the conclusion of the *Endeavour* expedition, Banks and Solander had amassed one of the largest botanical collections ever gathered during a sea voyage.

This marriage of wealth, science, art and ambition was a formula that Bligh respected and hoped to be part of in the *Bounty* voyage. Promotion and personal success depended on Bligh's ability to increase the number of discoveries that could be attributed to the wisdom and generosity of his patron.

From Bligh's writings and his experiments in planting gardens in places such as Adventure Bay, on the southern tip of Van Diemen's Land, we know he was more than a little interested in botanical science. These horticultural trials, his documentation of natural history phenomena and the ethnological comments in his logbook prior to the mutiny demonstrate Bligh's commitment to the precedent of scientific exploration established by Banks. His letter to Banks from Batavia, dated 13 October 1789, when Bligh was desperately ill with fever, shows how consumed the commander was with reassuring his patron that he had never neglected the finest principles throughout the voyage, and how keenly aware he was of the disappointment Banks would feel by news of the expedition's failure:

> *Had I been accidentally appointed to the command, the loss of the ship would give me no material concern; but when I reflect that it was through you, sir, who undertook to assert I was fully capable, and the eyes of every one regarding the progress of the voyage … I cannot say but it affects me considerably.*

Bligh was still trying to reconcile the mutiny with the accomplishment of a great part of his commission to load the *Bounty* with 'flourishing and fine' breadfruit plants and his personal challenge to keep the crew healthy:

> *To those, however, who may be disposed to blame, let them see I had in fact completed my undertaking. What man's situation could be so peculiarly flattering as mine*

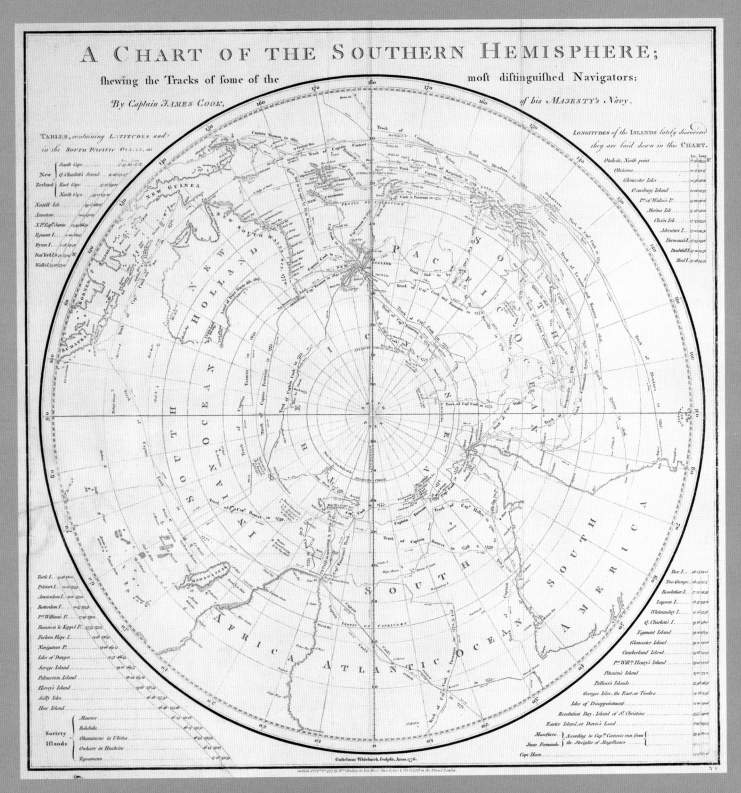

Cook's chart of the Southern Hemisphere, showing the voyages of some well-known navigators, 1777

Adventure Bay,
Van Diemen's Land,
where Bligh planted
a garden of fruit trees
and vegetables in 1788;
revisiting it in 1792, he
discovered that only one
apple tree had survived

View of Adventure Bay, Van Diemen's Land, New-Holland.

12 hours before the loss of the ship? Everything was in the most perfect order, and we were well stored with every necessary both for service and health ... the whole voyage was ¾ over, and the remaining part no way doubtful.

Banks was the powerful figure who would determine Bligh's future once he returned home. He also epitomised the ideal of eighteenth-century civilisation in terms of knowledge collected and analysed from new world exploration, a construct Bligh passionately wanted to play a part in. Because of his personal idolisation of Banks and fears for his own career prospects, it was extremely important to Bligh that he demonstrate his dedication to serving Banks' best interests. In naming the Banks Group of islands, Bligh was making both an apology and a commemorative gesture in the name of his patron.

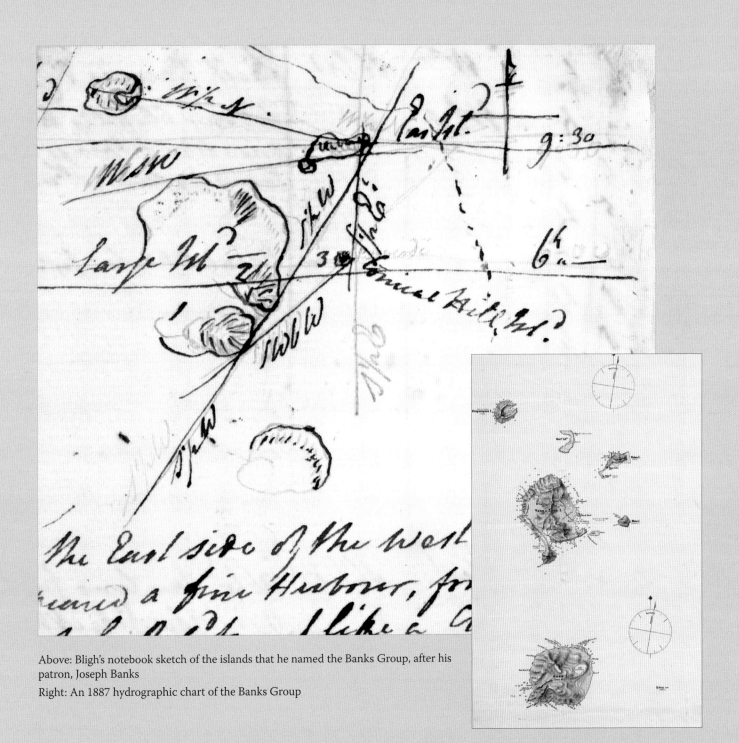

Above: Bligh's notebook sketch of the islands that he named the Banks Group, after his patron, Joseph Banks

Right: An 1887 hydrographic chart of the Banks Group

'Sea high—
Bailing & shiping water'
The travails of the journey

	K	F	Course	Wind	Rem.s Sund.y 17th May 1789 —
1	4		SWbW	WSW	Fresh Breezes & Cloudy. Steered
2	4			SW	N.º to counteract the Current.
3	4	6	"	"	Sea high – Bailing &
4	4	4			shiping Water.
5	4	6	"	"	
6	5	"	"	"	Bread & Water for Sup.r
7	3	4			
8	3	4	"	"	Storm.s of Thunder Light.g
9	3	4			& heavy Rain. —
10	3	4			Distress'd for want of light
11	3	4			to see our Course – No Stars
12	3	4			to be seen. —
1	4	4			
2	4	4			
3	4	4			
4	4	6			
5	5	4			
6	5	"			
7	4				D.º W.r Served a teaspoon full of
8	4				Rum & a morsel of Bread. —
9	4				Wet & Cold. —
10	3	4			Water spent almost on board
11	3	4			of us.
12	4	"			D.º W.r Sky dreadfully black
					all round us – Bread & a bit
	100				of Pork for Dinner. —
					Wet & Cold.
			NorW		

H	K	F	Courses	Wind	Rem^s Sund^y 17th May 1789—
1	4	—	SWbW	SEbS	Fresh Breezes & Cloudy. Steered SW to
2	4		SW		counteract the Current
3	4	6	"	"	Sea high—Bailing & shiping water.
4	4	4	"		
5	4	6	"	"	
6	5	"	"	"	Bread & Water for Sup [=Supper]
7	3	4			
8	3	4	"	"	Storms of Thunder Light^g & heavy
9	3	4			Rain.—
10	3	4			
11	3	4			Distress^d for want of light to see our
12	3	4			course—No Stars to be seen.—
1	4	4			
2	4	4			
3	4	4			
4	4	6			
5	5	"			
6	5	"			
7	4				
8	4				D^o W^r Served a teaspoonfull of Rum & a
9	4				morsel of Bread.—Wet & Cold.—
10	3	4			Water Spout almost on board of us.—
11	3	4			
12	4	"			

100
_____
No Obs^n

D^o W^r Sky dreadfully black all round us—
Bread & a ½ oz of Pork for Dinner.—
Wet & Cold.

The obvious challenge for Bligh as the launch pulled away from the *Bounty* was that of steering a course to safety. However, after Norton's death on Tofua, Bligh's mission became more complicated. Safety was not close at hand, and the nearest port where Bligh could hope to find a vessel in which to return to England was in Timor. So began the long journey and the rationing of food, intended to last for five days, into portions that could continue to feed the men for a potential journey of 50 days. To achieve this, the daily rations were calculated at the barest minimum to keep the men alive, and administered at eight in the morning, noon and sunset. Using his coconut-shell scales, Bligh weighed rations amounting to three fifths of an ounce of bread, a quarter of a pint of water (increased to three quarters of a pint a day, after rainfall) and a small portion of pork, varying from half an ounce to one ounce.

To maintain the regime, Bligh needed all his skill and knowledge of managing men at sea. One of the devices to make his own meal seem more substantial was to break his bread into small pieces and place it in the coconut shell holding his water ration. He would then drink the 'soup' with a spoon as slowly as possible to extend the illusion of a substantial meal. Contrary to the criticism of his ability to understand the responsibilities of naval command levelled at him by those historians who held Bligh's actions responsible for the mutiny, the voyage of the launch from Tofua to Timor proved beyond doubt that Bligh was a leader—if a troubled one. When the extreme weather became almost unbearable, Bligh would increase each man's portion with half a teaspoon of rum or a slightly larger morsel of pork.

Besides imposing rationing, there were other procedures Bligh needed to implement and enforce. Not least of these was the way in which to accommodate the 18 men in the small craft. To keep the launch stable, it was necessary for half of them to lie, inactive, on the bottom of the boat floor while the remainder sat. Changing shifts between those lying and those standing became part of the daily routine. Sleep was not a luxury enjoyed by anyone, as time recumbent was spent more in a stupor than in repose.

Bligh wrote that they frequently had to bail all night to avoid being swamped and capsizing. In his log, he notes on 20 May that 'What little sleep we get is in the midst of water, and we wake with Severe Cramps and Pains in our Bones'.

Routine was the key to maintaining order and sanity amongst the men and, to this end, Bligh devised employment for them. His aim was to divert his crew from falling into despondency

Bligh found flying fish in the stomachs of two boobies caught on 27 May

One crew member
bailing water, another
preparing to use
the logline and two
working the sail

A model of the launch with each man performing
an activity recorded by Bligh during the voyage

if they began to doubt that their course was leading to a port. Construction of the logline was the first of these measures, and all the men were drilled in the method for counting seconds accurately so that they might calculate the distance covered each day with greater precision. The log was thrown overboard hourly, on a daily basis, and this task helped create a rhythm, marking the real passage of time and distance. Bligh's need to take observations at noon when the sun was over the meridian was another activity that often required assistance in order to keep him raised high enough in the vessel and braced securely against the often rough seas to make his sighting. These were the markers in about one thousand hours of endurance experienced by those in the launch as they journeyed some 4000 miles at four and a fifth miles per hour and 100 miles per day.

Being without firearms, Bligh knew that he could not risk another landing on an inhabited island. He noted in his letter to Banks describing the voyage that, on 7 May, they 'discovered other Islands' and were 'chased by Two large Cannoes, but got clear of them by Rowing'.

It was a repeated dilemma for the party that the fertile islands with the promise of fresh food and of sleep on dry land were too dangerous to risk anchoring near.

The beaker, which is only 5.4 x 4.8 centimetres, that Bligh used to measure the daily water allowance

From 10 May onwards, the weather deteriorated into torrential rain, thunder and severe lightning, gales and high seas. The occupants of the launch were perpetually wet and severely affected by the cold, frequently reporting aching bones to Bligh. While the constant dousing possibly staved off dehydration for the men, there was a ceaseless demand to bail the vessel and the risk of hypothermia was high. Bligh hit upon the clever idea of systematically stripping off clothing and rinsing, then wringing the items out in the sea, which was considerably warmer than the icy rainfall. In this manner, he documented that they were frequently 'refreshed', although he conceded that soon there was little fabric left to wring out. Bligh's log entry for 17 May offers this description:

> At Noon a water Spout was very near on board of us. I issued an ounce of Pork, in addition to the allowance of Bread and jill of water; but before we began to eat, every person striped and wrung their cloaths through the Sea water, which we found warm and refreshing.

While the rainfall kept their water supply adequate, the storms made navigation difficult, and Bligh was constantly afraid that his sightings at noon were badly impaired by the difficulty he had in sighting the sun. Strong gales and blinding rain meant high seas, and the launch was forced to run with the prevailing seas to avoid capsizing. On 22 May, fleshing out his entries in the notebook, Bligh records in his logbook:

> *Our Situation to day highly perilous ... We were obliged to take the Course of the Sea, running right before it and breaking all over us. Watching with the utmost care, as the least error in the Helm would in a moment be our destruction.*

This loss of control was agonising for Bligh after his meticulous calculations but, once the gale had passed, he returned the vessel to its course.

As the men approached the coast of New Holland, seabirds became more common and the crew was able to catch several and eat them raw after dividing the catch and distributing the pieces by means of the game, 'Who shall have this?', described earlier (see page 50). Bligh describes catching two boobies on 27 May: 'their Stomachs contained several Flying Fish and squids, all of which I saved to be divided for dinner'.

Once the storms had abated, the weather became insufferably hot and, without any protection from the sun, the men were stricken with heat stroke and lay in a debilitating lethargy. In the nick of time for the survival of some of the crew, the launch came within sight of a reef and managed to navigate a passage through it into calm water. Bligh, in his report to Banks, expressed his conviction that the six days that the party spent amongst the coral islands near the Great Barrier Reef saved the party by providing an opportunity for sleep and meals of berries, beans, oysters and clams. This sojourn had trials of its own, as Bligh was nearly faced with another mutiny, but this adventure is discussed later (see page 143).

On 17 May, Bligh recorded the appearance of a waterspout that nearly overwhelmed the launch

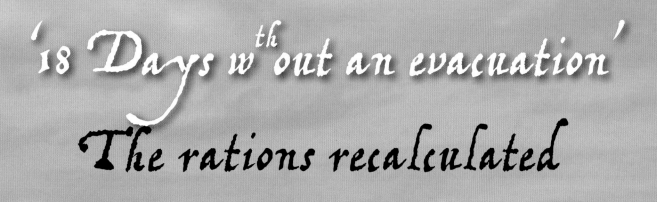

'18 Days wth out an evacuation'
The rations recalculated

H	K	F	Courses	Winds	Remarks Monday 25 May 1789
1	4	6	WbS	NNE	Fine Wr & cool Air — some
2	4				Boobies — Men of War Birds Rk
3	4				Chicken. —
4	4				Overhauled our Bread & found
5	4	4			43 days Bread at the rate of
6	4	4			weight of 2 Musket Balls, or
7	4	4			1/12 of a lb to each Man pr Day
8	4	4			Saw a Gannet. —
9	4	2			Our Allowance now will be 1/12
10	4	4			of lb Bread & a small Wine
11	5				Glass of Water at Breakfast &
12	5				Dinner. & only Water at Sup-
1	4				per. —
2	4				Every one complains of Costive
3	4	4			ness most of 10 Days without
4	4	4			an evacuation by
5	4				
6	4				Caught a Noddy by Hand
7	5				
8	4	4			Flying showers of Rain
9	5				Bread for Breakfast
10	5				
11	5				
12	5				Squally. Noddies & Tropic
					Birds/

Latd: 19:32 St

H	K	F	Courses	Wind	Rem^s Mond^y 25 May 1789
1	4	6	WbS	SSE	Fine W^r & a Cool Air—Some Boobies—Men of War Birds [=frigatebirds]—MK Chicken [=storm petrel].—
2	4				
3	4				
4	4				Overhauled our Bread & found 43 days Bread at the rate of weight of 2 Musket Balls, or $^1/_{12}$ of a lb to each Man p^r Day.
5	4	4			
6	4	4			
7	4	4	"		Saw a Gannet.—
8	4	4	"		our Issues now will be $^1/_{12}$ of lb Bread & a small Wine Glass of Water at Breakfast & Dinner & only Water at Supper.—
9	4	2			
10	4	4			
11	5				
12	5				
1	4				Every one complains of Costiveness most of us 18 Days wthout an evacuation—
2	4				
3	4	4			
4	4	4			
5	4				Caught a Noddy by Hand
6	4				
7	5				
8	4	4			Flying showers of Rain
9	5				Bread for Breakfast
10	5				
11	5				
12	5				Squally. Noddies & Tropic Gulls

Lat^d 13°.32' S

During the 14 days of sailing from the Banks Group of islands through the Coral Sea towards the Great Barrier Reef (south of Endeavour reef), the weather became very severe, making steering and navigation extremely difficult. For four days in succession the sun was invisible at noon and, at other times, the sea was so rough that Bligh's calculations of latitude could not have been accurate. The launch ran with the prevailing wind, fortunately a strong easterly, and, even with the sails reefed, the vessel continued to make progress in the general direction the crew wished to take.

On 24 May, Bligh was alarmed by the effect of the weather and decided to reduce the rations to ensure that the small reserve of food would not be exhausted if the launch should miss Timor and be forced to sail on to Java. He commented in the notebook that the new rations would be one twelfth of a pound of bread and a small wine glass of water at breakfast and only water at supper. Not surprisingly, by now all the occupants of the launch were suffering from what Bligh described as 'costiveness'—constipation and the resulting crippling pain in their bowels—through the lack of fibre in their diet. Some relief was afforded after this decision to reduce rations by the catching of two boobies, which were dismembered and distributed according to the 'Who shall have this?' game.

The bullet pendant that Bligh used as a weight to measure the men's daily ration of bread

It is instructive to consider the kind of rations an eighteenth-century sailor could usually expect and to remember how aware Bligh had been on the *Bounty* about the connection between good food and good health, and how regular meals influenced morale. On a normal voyage, each man was allocated a pound of ships biscuit per day, four pounds of beef, two pounds of pork, two pounds of peas, one and a half pounds of oatmeal, six ounces of sugar and butter and 12 ounces of cheese per week. Other provisions were substituted as necessary. The purser purchased fresh vegetables when they could be procured in a port at a reasonable price. All food onboard a sailing vessel was stored in casks in the hold and the bread and biscuits kept in sacks in the bread room. (Baked biscuit could keep for up to a year.) Meat was cut into small pieces and preserved with salt. Meals were washed down with a daily allowance of one gallon of beer or the equivalent. On voyages south of the latitude of Lisbon, Portugal, foods were chosen that were less likely to spoil in the heat. It was a common practice on extended voyages for the crew to supplement their meat intake by catching rats, skinning them and selling them to each other.

The coconut bowl on which Bligh carved his name, the date and the words:
'the cup I eat my miserable allowance out of'

Bligh referred to storm petrels as MK Chickens or Mother Carey's Chickens, as was the custom of eighteenth-century mariners, who believed that they were an omen of bad weather

Gould; Birds of Australia, fol., vol. vii. pl. 62.
(Untitled Plate 26)

Thalassidroma melanogastra, Gould.
Black-bellied Storm Petrel.

Gould; Handbook, Birds Australia vol 2 p. 479
Sp. 667, Pagella melanogaster.

The figures represent the birds of the natural size inhabiting the different temperatures seas which so frequently occur in high southern latitudes

Water was difficult to keep fresh and, within less than a month of leaving port, the water would begin to taste bad. It was often filtered through a dripstone, an innovation introduced to ship life by Bligh, providing some improvement to the taste and quality. Rum was the more popular beverage, and the strength of ships' rum was notorious. It was commonly watered down before distribution but, even so, remained potent enough to sedate or inflame sailors depending on their mood. Bligh knew how to administer alcohol to best effect in the launch, using rum to lift the spirits in times of intense cold and saving his small quantity of wine to produce when crew members became dangerously ill and weak.

Years after the voyage, Bligh would recount the feelings of revulsion he experienced when presented with the oily bit of stomach he 'won' in a game of 'Who shall have this?' Historian Greg Dening has calculated the total food allocation for each man in the launch for the 47-day trip as: seven pounds of bread, one pound of salted pork, one pint of rum, five ounces of wine, two and a quarter coconuts, one banana, one pint of coconut milk, one and a quarter raw seabirds, and four ounces of fish. While camped on the New Holland coast, each man ate four pints of oysters and clams, some unspecified amount of cabbage palm, berries and wild peas. The daily calorie count of a sailor's rations on a normal voyage would be 4450. Dening, with the aid of a nutritionist, has determined that those in the launch would have survived on 345 calories per day—a deficit of 4105 calories and an associated total weight loss for the journey's duration of roughly 56 pounds. The men suffered agonising cramps and rheumatic pains in their bones, probably largely due to vitamin C deficiency.

Bligh's coconut shell bowl

In his logbook account, Bligh made a point of discussing the possibility that the party in the launch might have considered cannibalism and vehemently stated that he could see no reason why any in the party would come to this way of thinking. He wrote that he felt no 'extreme hunger or thirst. My allowance satisfies me, knowing I can have no more'. The heart of Bligh's successful regime of rationing lies in his essential, scrupulous fairness and his contentment when the boundaries of authority were clear. Everyone in the launch knew that Bligh ate and drank a ration that was no different to that of any other man. It was the blend of leadership and fairness that enabled him to write that he had 'surmounted the difficulties and distresses of a most perilous voyage and arrived safely in an hospitable port'.

'fell in with a reef
wch broke dreadfully'

Clearing the reef

I now expected to fall in with New Holl^d
reef every hour, being determind to look for a
passage & take the first opening. — At 1 am fell
in with a reef wch hope dreadfully but we were
so providentially situated that with clearing
with risk or trouble. — I stood however
all night to the N.W. & at day light
steered in to determine whether the reef
was detached or a part of the main reef.
At 9 made faund the main reef & dis^dc
an opening ¾ mile wide. Stood for it wth a
strong current set N. & West. — When in the
passage land like an isl^d was only seen
& bore W ¼ N. The reef to the north^d inclined
to the N.E. & to the South W ¼ SW & blue water
to the North as far as I could see — Deep
water in the Channel. — More land seen
& mountainous. Endeavour to come to a
Grapnel on the Reef but could not the
current run so strong to the West. I therefore
bore away as I could not keep my ground
to observe. — All happy at this providential
entry. — Expected to take the reef No
any ground inside reef.
The land first seen & the north^d in sight
both still look like isl^d but perhaps joined
by low land — Too hazy to see the land to the South
Smooth water

28 May 1789

H	K	F	Course	Wind	Remarks
6	4	"	"	"	At 6 Steered again for the Coast.—
7	3	4	W½N	"	Nothing insight.—
8	4	"	"	"	
9	3	"	"	"	
10	2	"	NNE		Made the Reef from NNW to SbW & Saw a Hill Dis^t back WbN—Hauled
	1	4	} W½N		Wind—Saw an opening ^h9½ steered in
11	5	"	} WNW	"	W½N & Land only seen as before W½N
12	4	"	NW	E	8 leg^s ½ Mile across.—

Saw Land High SWbW

At 11 Bore away—Chan^l ESE 5 Miles. Land SWbW to NWbW Land first Seen WbS

Lat^d Obs^d 12°.46'   At Noon Fine W^r Land first seen WSW 5 or 6 leag^s & Land farther North NWbW½W

I now expected to fall in with New Holl reefs every hour being determined to look for a passage & take the first opening.—At 1 am fell in with a reef wch broke dreadfully but we were so providentially situated that with cleared with risk or trouble [possibly Bligh meant 'we cleared without risk or trouble'].— I stood however allnight to the NNE & at day light steered in to determine whether the Reef was detached or a part of the Main Reef At 9^h made the Main Reef & disc. an opening ½ Mile wide. Stood for it wth a strong current setting West.—When in the Passage Land like an Isl^d was only seen & bore W½N—The Reef to the north^d inclined to the NE & to the South SSW & blue water to the North as far as I could see—Deep water in the Channel—More land Seen & mountainous. I endeavor^d to Come to a Grapnel on the Reef but could not the Current run so Strong to the south. I therefore bore away as I could not keep my ground to observe.—All happy at this Providential entry.—Expected to take the Reef—No dry ground inside Reef. The land first seen & the north insight both still look like Isl^ds but perhaps joined by lowland—too hazy to see the land to the South Smooth water

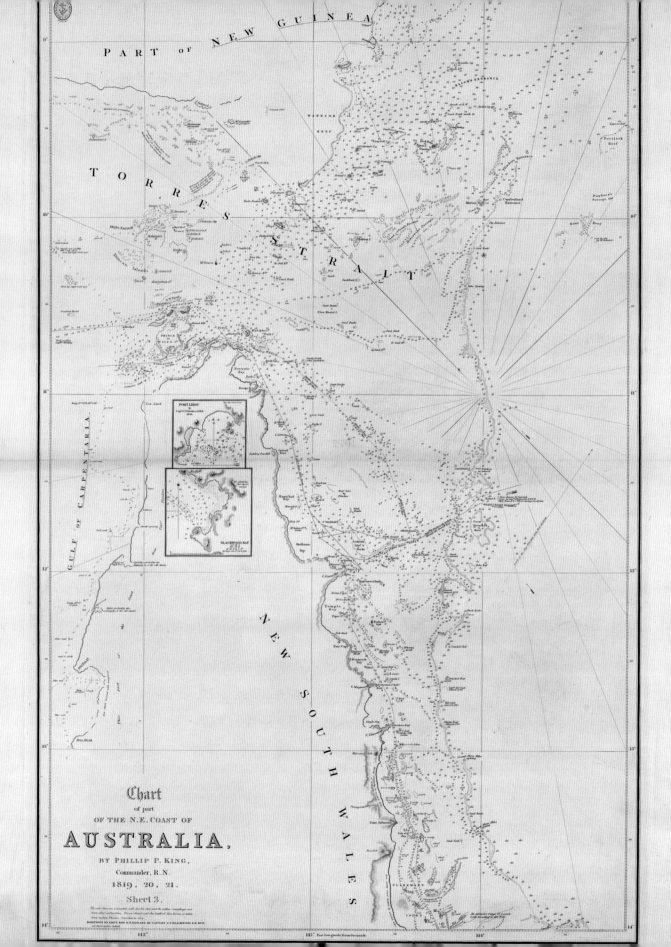

Chart
of part
OF THE N.E. COAST OF
AUSTRALIA,
BY PHILLIP P. KING,
Commander, R.N.
1819, 20, 21.
Sheet 3.

*I*n the early hours of 28 May, those awake in the launch heard the roar of breakers as they approached the 'Reefs of new Holland'. In his narrative of the launch voyage, Fryer is contemptuous of Bligh's perceived fear at the sound of the waves, and Bligh, in his report to Banks, makes much of the rough and unpredictable seas that he battled to keep the launch safely clear of the reef and certain destruction. Fryer and Bligh had reached a state of mutual dislike onboard the *Bounty* prior to the mutiny. This situation had been exacerbated at Adventure Bay when Fryer was humiliated in front of the entire crew after Bligh, having accused him of misconduct in relation to the *Bounty*'s account books, forced him to sign the ledgers. Fryer could see no heroism in the actions of a man who had resorted to such publicly punitive measures.

It is not surprising then that Fryer's version of events presents Bligh as overreacting and in need of his practical advice. In comparison, Bligh's account makes no mention of any assistance of any kind from his master or other members of the crew in either holding the launch clear of the breakers until daybreak or in locating the entrance through the reef into the calm waters beyond. Writing to Banks, Bligh describes the midnight incident:

> *I fell in with most dreadful Breakers, but I was able to stand clear of them ... At 9 in the morning I saw the Reef again, and soon after standing along it to the Northward I discovered an Opening, which I safely entered and got into Smooth Water.*

In Fryer's description, the other sailors are acknowledged and the credit for entering into the calm waters inside the reef is shared. Bligh is depicted as panicking and shouting out predictions of disaster while Fryer describes soothing the crew in order to pull the launch to safety:

> *We got the sail dip very well and Boat haul'd on a wind—and then got our oars out and pull'd but in the height of this [?] Captn Bligh calld out Pull my lads we shall be Swamp'd ... I then calld out my lads Pull there is no danger ...*

Fryer goes on to explain that he was standing in the stern of the launch, looking ahead, when Bligh asked him if he could see an entrance:

> *I said yes sir I see a place where there is no Breakers—he came forward himself and saw the same place I did ... when we came in to it we found that providence had guided us into one of the finest Harbour mouths that Possible could be ...*

The north-east coast of New Holland where, in rough seas, Bligh battled to keep the launch clear of the reefs; he eventually found a passage through the reef near Cape Weymouth

A page from the original manuscript of John Fryer's narrative

These differing accounts are a reminder of Bligh's control of the official records of the voyage, and his refusal to allow Fryer access to writing materials to use in the launch. Both Bligh's notebook and his logbook maintain the detached tone of formal naval records, and are written by the superior officer, whereas Fryer's account is written by a subordinate officer who voices the discontent of the crew. While Bligh is matter of fact in his comments about clearing the reef to escape the ravages of the open sea, Fryer, in less polished and more emotional language, reveals the relief of the sailors as they reached the temporary haven beyond the treacherous surf:

> I will leave the reader to judge what feelings a set of poor fellows must have had at such a time as this as I have not words to express myself.

At this time, Bligh was the undisputed commander but, in Fryer's account, there are hints of the dissatisfaction that erupted when the boat reached Restoration Island. Comparing the two versions emphasises that they are not written transcripts of the conversations that occurred in the course of the daily sailing routines. They are documents that have been edited and carefully constructed for an audience. Bligh's notebook and logbook are unlike the modern aircraft black box that records the conversations of the pilot and crew. Allowing for the possible exaggerations in Fryer's narrative, based on his dislike of Bligh,

John Fryer, the *Bounty*'s master, who wrote his own account of the voyage in the launch

Detail of Bligh's
notebook entry for
28 May 1789

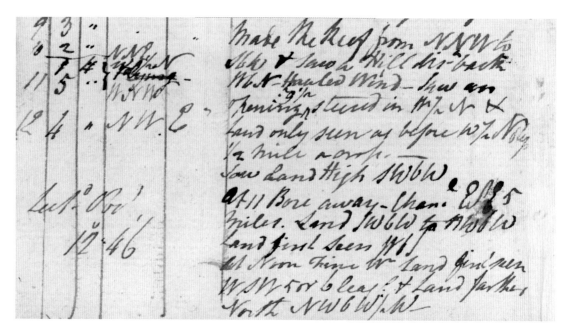

his account of clearing the reef describes the crew in action as the seasoned sailors they were, despite their greatly weakened condition. Bligh rarely admits the crew into his narrative as anything but passive dependants.

As the launch passed through the opening in the reef and into the sheltered waters within, all onboard were relieved in anticipation of landing and the opportunity to rest and find fresh food and water.

Thus appears the only land insight & nearest to the Channel when we were within the Entrance bears. WbN to NbW

When Bligh comments in his notebook on 28 May that the 'land first seen ... look like Isl^{ds} but perhaps joined by lowland', he could be referring to Cape Direction and Cape Weymouth; his entry is followed by this sketch of Cape Direction and the land immediately to the south

'The Kangooro's I beleive swim from ... Isl^d to Isl^d'

Restoration Island

I now have 38 days Allowance
Bread at 1/12 lb ℗ day

Saw many Pieces of Pumice stone
on the Shore & a very long & large Tree
hove up at the back of the Beach
From whence I conclude Gales are strong
when they blow from the N^o

Our little Well still supplies
plenty of Water. —

Emp^d a Hand mend^g the Main Sail

Saw a Bee & some Lizards. —

What Beaches we see are of a White
Sand. —

The Kangoroo's I beleive swim from
the Main from Isl^d to Isl^d —

All the Country we can see appeared
rather scorched — But a pleasing variety
of high & low land & the interior part of
the Main Mountainous

This Isl^d may be known by a heap
of large Rocks which form round Top Isl^d
that lies ¾ mile to the E^NE of it.

I find the Lat^d of Restoration
Point to be 12:39 S 144:44 E

30 May 1789

The little pork I had when we sailed we have found frequently to be stolen & found it so now, but cannot discover the Wretch that did it.—

Kind providence protects us wonderfully but it is a most unhappy situation to be in a Boat among such discontented People who dont know what to be at or what is best for them.

High Water at Noon ab^t 3 feet rise

55:23	Sun Alt LL
— 4	Error
55:19	
13	
55:32	
34.28	
21:49	
12.39	Lat^d of Restoration Point.

I now have 38 days allowance Bread at $^1/_{12}$ lb p^r days.

Saw many Pieces of Pumice Stone on the Shore & a very long & large Tree hove up at the back of the Beach from whence I conclude Gales are strong when they blow from the NW

our little well still supplies plenty of Water.—

Empl^d a Hand mend^g the Main Sail

Saw a Bee & some Lizards.—

What Beaches we see are of a white Sand.—

The Kangooro's I beleive swim from the Main from Isl^d to Isl^d—

All the country we can see appeared rather scorched—But a pleasing variety of high & low land & the interior part of the Main Mountainous

This Isl^d may be known by a heap of large Rocks which form round Top Isl^d that lies ¼ Mile to the ESE of it.

I find the Lat^d of Restoration Point to be 12°:39'S 144°:44' E^t—

THE KANGUROO.

On 29 May, the launch landed on an island inside the sheltered waters protected by the reef. Bligh named the place Restoration Island, as the date was the anniversary of the Restoration of Charles II, and the island offered a restoration of hope for survival for the weakened party. They landed at 5.15 pm, ate some oysters from the rocks and, for the first time, divided the party between the boat and the shore so that all the men could rest at the same time.

Fryer's narrative provides a description of the first excursions to gather food:

> but this time we could see that there was no Natives near us I set out in company with Messrs Peckover Nelson Cole and several more—to get oysters. after we had got as many as four or five could carry, Mr Peckover & Mr Cole and two or three more carry them to the Boat and the rest stay'd to get more.

Bligh enforced the notion of communal eating and centralised water storage. In the account he sent to Banks, Bligh describes the good supplies of water and oysters they found and how these were combined to make 'very good Stews'. With his small magnifying glass, described as 'my reading Glass', Bligh was able to light a fire.

In his *Narrative of the Mutiny*, Bligh describes the berries on the island in detail, revealing his keen botanical interests and relying on his vivid memories of their appearance:

> One sort grew on a small delicate kind of vine; they were the size of a large gooseberry, and very like in substance, but had only a sweet taste; the skin was a pale red, streaked with yellow the long way of the fruit: it was pleasant and agreeable. Another kind grew on bushes, like that which is called the sea-side grape in the West Indies; but the fruit

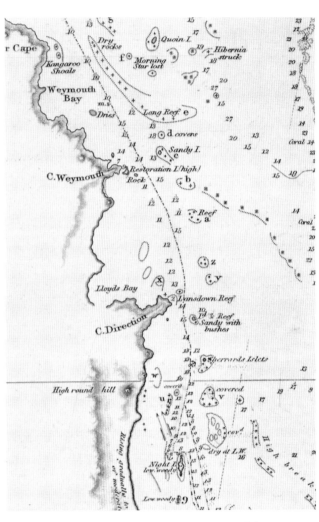

A section of the map on page 122, the first detailed chart that shows Restoration Island named

An illustration of a kangaroo in the 1820 publication, *Dangerous Voyage of Captain Bligh in an Open Boat ... in the Year 1789* by William Bligh

Bligh's men found weapons on Restoration Island, indicating the presence of Aboriginal people

was very different, and more like elder-berries, growing in clusters in the same manner. The third sort was a black berry, not in such plenty as the others, and resembled a bullace, or large kind of sloe, both in size and taste.

Bligh also explains how he made the decision to allow the party to eat the berries after observing birds consuming them in large quantities.

While the island offered sanctuary from their ordeal, in reality the men were far from safe. There was evidence of the presence of Aboriginal people, and Bligh was anxious about a possible confrontation that he believed they could not survive without firearms. The men found implements like the ones they had discovered in Adventure Bay: 'a pointed stick, about three feet long, with a slit in the end of it, to sling stones with, the same as the natives of Van Diemen's land use', and Bligh found 'two wigwams'. Kangaroo tracks and a snake skeleton on a tree branch were evidence of wild animals that could attract hunters to the island. As a cautionary measure, Bligh ordered that no large fires should be made, but a spark that started a brush fire caused him great consternation and resulted in one of his terrible rages. To quell the fire, the men had to quickly pull out the grass growing in its path.

Fryer makes further reference to Bligh's bad temper and his report of conversations illustrates the conflict that persisted between Bligh and the men:

> When Messrs Cole and Peckover return'd I ask them how those came on that remain at the Boat, they said that Captn Bligh was in a sad passion calling every Body the Name that he could think of telling them—that if it had not been for him that they would not a been there.

At this juncture, some officers held Bligh completely responsible for creating the situation that had forced them to leave the safety of the *Bounty* with him:

> Poor Mr Nelson whom I very seldom heard swear—said to me Yes Damn his blood it is his Oeconomy that brought us here.

An incident that greatly affected Bligh at this time was curiously not recorded in the notebook, but does receive detailed attention in his *Narrative*. On the first night in their safe anchorage, one of the gudgeons (a metal plate carrying the eye for the pin of the rudder) fell off and disappeared. Bligh had been extremely worried about the risk of this occurring and had fitted 'grummets' for oars to be used in the event of its collapse, but he knew that if the gudgeon gave way at sea, the launch would very likely have skewed in the waves and overturned:

> It appears, therefore, a providential circumstance, that it happened at this place, and was in our power to remedy the defect; for by great good luck we found a large staple in the boat that answered the purpose.

He was so moved by the incident that he spent the next day sitting at a distance from his men, in isolation, 'correcting the Books', but also writing a new prayer which he inscribed

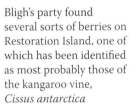

Bligh's party found several sorts of berries on Restoration Island, one of which has been identified as most probably those of the kangaroo vine, *Cissus antarctica*

The first of three pages of a prayer that Bligh wrote in the notebook

in his notebook so that he could refer to it every morning and evening. The first page of the prayer reads:

O Lord our heavenly Father almighty and everlasting God, who has safely brought us to the beginning of this day; In and through the merits of our blessed Saviour through whom we are taught to ask all things,—We thy unworthy Servants prostrate ourselves before thee & humbly ask thee forgiveness of our sins and Transgressions

We most devoutly thank thee for our preservation & are truly conscious that only through thy Divine Mercy we have been saved—We supplicate thy Glorious Majesty to accept our unfeigned Prayers & Thanksgivings for thy gracious Protection.—Thou hast shewed us wonders in the Deep, that we might see how powerfull & gracious a God thou art; how able & ready to help those who trust in thee.

Thou hast given us strength & fed us & hast shewn how both Winds & Seas obey thy command, that we may learn …

The prayer perhaps is more evidence of Bligh's patronising attitude towards his men and his need to remain in absolute control. It is also a written meditation reaffirming the purpose for continuing with the dangerous voyage for which there were no guarantees of a happy ending. At this point, Bligh felt the need not only to amend the books that would be read by his superiors and his patron, but also to balance the books with God, thanking the Creator for His mercy so far and beseeching divine protection for the remaining trials ahead.

That Bligh remained alert and highly observant is attested to by the detailed account of his sojourn on the island in his *Narrative*. While, in his version, Fryer remembers Bligh as very difficult and temperamental, Bligh was able, for better or worse, to temporarily block out recollections of the human dilemmas and to reproduce the natural beauties of Restoration Island. In this excerpt, Bligh the naturalist and solitary explorer is revealed:

> *The shore of this island is very rocky, except the part we landed at, and here I picked up many pieces of pumice-stone. On the part of the main next to us were several sandy bays, but at low-water they became an extensive rocky flat. The country had rather a barren appearance, except in a few places where it was covered with wood. A remarkable range of rocks lay a few miles to the SW, or a high peaked hill terminated the coast towards the sea, with other high lands and islands to the southward. A high fair cape showed the direction of the coast to the NW, about seven leagues, and two small isles lay three or four leagues to the northward.*
>
> *I saw a few bees or wasps, several lizards, and the blackberry bushes were full of ants nests, webbed as a spider's, but so close and compact as not to admit the rain.*

The sojourn on Restoration Island was a brief two days and, as the party departed, armed Aboriginal people appeared on the mainland beach, shouting and gesturing. Fearing canoes, Bligh did not hesitate and headed north towards Fair Cape.

'*Parties return'd ... with some fine Oysters & Clams*'
Sunday Island

Canoe ab. 33 feet long bottom up made
of three pieces with a sharp head a little
carved in resemblance of a Fishes head
& three feet wide — I suppose would carry
20 Men —

All the Country is like Dampiers descrip-
of it. This W.d of a Moderate height very
Rocky & only Shrubs & wire Grass.
The Tide appears to rise here about 4 or
5 feet. — I went on the heights but
saw no land more to the North than West
Several Isld.s lay to the E & S.E. & one N.W.

Parties return'd at Noon with some fine
~~Boat~~ Oysters & Clams & Dog Fish — Squibs. —
Began to Cook Dinner

At Noon I found by Good Observation
the lat.e of this place 11°.50' N.o & Long.o by
Acc.t — 141°.29' — A Tide or Current has
set in our favor 17 Miles North & a little
Westerly —

31 May 1789 _____

At day light I found the appearance of the country all changed being all low,
some nothing but white Sand Hills & the rest not a very fertile appearance
however there were in many places Trees & small Wood.
Several Isl^ds now lay to the North & East and I took a channel between the
nearest & the Main ab^t 1 Mile across leaving the Isl^ds on the Starb^d Side—some
of these were very pretty Spots & well situated for Fish many of which we sailed
through but could catch none.— Seven natives now made their appearance on
the Main Armed with a Spear & another weapon. They made signs to come
on shore but as my situation was not elligible I did not choose—They waved
branches of some Tree or Bush as sign of Friendship but there were some of their
other motions less friendly.—A larger Party we saw coming from a dis^t. back
I therefore steered on for an Isl^d farther off bear^g
At 8 O'Clock we landed to get what the Isl^d produced—From whence the
Main bore WbN 3 leag^s to S½E 4 Miles full of Milk white sand Hills—
No mountainous land to be seen at the back.—
The Natives were jet Black & seemed to have rather bushy hair or wool. I do
not think their talk or voice was like Van Diemens land inhabitants.—
Two Isl^ds lay off the North part of the Main in sight.—
The Isl^ds in general are from ½ Mile Round to ab^t 2 Miles.—
Found water in Hollow & an old Cannoe ab^t 33 feet long bottom up made
of three pieces with a sharp head a little carved in resemblance of a Fishes
head—& three feet wide—I suppose would carry 20 Men—
All the Country is like Dampiers descrip^s of it.—
This Isl^d of a Moderate height very Rocky & only Shrubs & wire Grass.
The Tide appears to rise here about 4 or 5 feet.—I went on the heights but
saw no land more to the North than WbN Several Isld^s lay to the E & SE &
some NWbN
Parties return'd at Noon with some fine Oysters & Clams & Dog Fish—
Squibs [=squids].—
Began to Cook Dinner
At Noon I found by Good Observation the lat^d of this place 11°58' S^O & Long^d
by Acc^t—144°.29' E^t—A Tide or Current has set in our favor 17 Miles North a
little Westerly—

Forbes Island. E. C. A.
H. M. S. "Salamander" December 20th 1864.

Dunk Island. west. East Coast of Australia.

Holborne Island. north. East Coast of Australia.

Sunday Island. East Coast Australia

*I*n Bligh's notebook, the entries for Sunday 31 May consist of navigational calculations and brief observations about sailing conditions and the quantities of birds and fish. Bligh omitted all references to an incident that could almost have become a second mutiny. The fact that he did not mention the matter suggests that he realised he had behaved inappropriately and wanted to forget the incident as soon as it had concluded. Later, when he recollected the incident in his *Narrative of the Mutiny*, Bligh twisted the sequence of events, accusing Purcell, the carpenter, of laziness. Bligh revisited the altercation in his logbook; Fryer also described the events in his narrative of the launch voyage.

The party had landed on Sunday Island to gather clams or oysters. Fryer suggested that, as some of the men had been less diligent in collecting oysters at their last landfall, on this occasion each man should eat what he collected. When Elphinstone, master's mate, stated that he would rather stay in the boat than look for food, this behaviour sparked Fryer to remark that they were all equally fatigued, so each man should provide for himself. According to Fryer's narrative, Bligh agreed that 'what every man put into the kittle should take the same Quantity out'.

The men divided into three parties, and Purcell was the first to fill his bag and return to the boat, thinking that he had his own meal ready to eat. Bligh, however, demanded that all the oysters be placed in a communal pot; at that, Purcell refused. Bligh interpreted this act as insubordination and called Purcell a 'damned scoundrel', adding, 'If I had not brought you here, you would have all perished'. Purcell's response was 'Yes, sir, if it had not been for you we should not have been here'. Incensed, Bligh once again called him a scoundrel, to which Purcell replied, 'I am not a scoundrel, sir … I am as good a man as you in that respect'. This was too much for Bligh. As he firmly believed that the only way to conclude the voyage successfully was for him to remain in complete, undisputed control, he interpreted Purcell's remark about equality as meaning that he was just as fit to command the party as Bligh. Flying into a rage, Bligh drew his cutlass and told the carpenter to take another cutlass to fight out the claim to the death. Purcell quickly conceded that he would not take up a cutlass against his officer. At this point, Fryer writes that he could not help laughing 'to see Captn Bligh swaggering with a cutlass over the carpenter's head', and he promptly intervened, calling out: 'No fighting here—I put you both under an arrest'. Further angered and outraged, Bligh turned on Fryer, making it clear that he would violently resist any such efforts and treat them

Sketch of four islands, including Sunday Island, off the east coast of Australia

The men had with them in the launch four cutlasses, one of which Bligh brandished in rage when his authority was challenged by Purcell in an incident on Sunday Island that could have escalated into another mutiny

as mutinous actions to be punished accordingly. Purcell managed to explain himself adequately; whereupon Bligh asked his pardon and the matter subsided.

Did Bligh overreact? If a similar incident had occurred at sea, Bligh would have had support from his officers and alternative punishments at hand to discipline a subordinate for refusing to follow his commands, however contradictory they might have seemed to his men. With the perpetual complaining of his men about their hunger, their physical agonies and the pleas for increased rations, not to mention his own privations, it was not surprising that Bligh, never known for his patience, should be unable to take a benevolent view of disobedience. The party was still on a naval expedition and he was the appointed commander who must retain his authority. In Bligh's view, this was no place for a discussion about the equality of souls or the rights of every man to be treated alike. It was Bligh's chance to salvage some vestiges of glory from saving the *Bounty* loyalists. He also hoped to preserve his natural history observations and geographic discoveries and to present them to the English scientific community. Bligh was going to remain leader even if it meant killing members of the party.

Later, Bligh privately chastised Fryer for his behaviour, but the master could not remain silent and expostulated that, in taking up the cutlass, Bligh had reduced himself to the same level of uncivilised behaviour as Purcell. In his narrative, Fryer reports his response:

> there [are] other methods in making people do as they were ordered, without fighting them, that he might rest assur'd that I would support him in that as far as was in my power.

On Sunday Island, the men searched for food, returning to the boat with dogfish, as well as oysters, clams and squids

This self-righteous remark might well have inflamed Bligh to respond with some undocumented expletives.

In his description of events, Bligh called it 'a tumult which lasted about a quarter of an hour' and, in a summation that is unintentionally funny given the magnitude of the disturbance, he writes, 'I did not suffer this to interfere with the harmony of the well disposed'. With the long, desperate struggle up the coast of New Holland, round the tip of Cape York Peninsula and on through heavy seas to Coupang, harmony amongst the crew members was perhaps a slight overstatement, but Bligh was determined to present the voyage in the way in which he thought it should have unfolded.

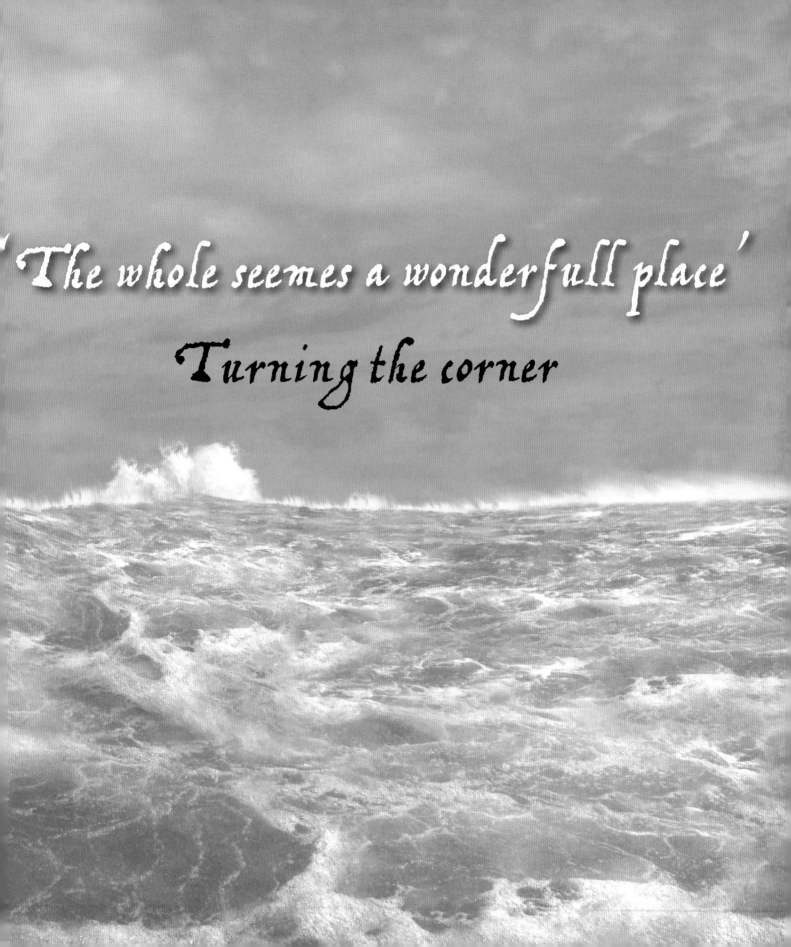

'The whole seemes a wonderfull place'

Turning the corner

It appeared as a Parcel of High Islands
which might from the appearance of it
be called the Bay of Islands. But I
believe they may all join by low land. —
More Land was now seen ahead. and
small Keys to the NW taking the direction as if the Boundary of the Reef was
such — The Country now seems to be
rocky & no Sand Hills

At 11 the Main appeared to be broken & formed
deep Inlets & M't Isld more considerable
than what we have seen & some very high
appeared in the N. & NW. — The whole seemes
a wonderfull place — I do not imagine that
any of the Isld are joined by Reefs; if I may
Judge from those I've seen we now pass
several between me & the Main, & others are
constantly appearing. —

At Noon discovered a Reef extends from SWest
to NE whether this reef joins round to the S.
I cannot say or whether it is connected to some
more to the North. Some small Keys, I could
just see in the Range of the Reef & therefore perhaps
the High Isld to the north, are not connected
with it. —

3 June 1789

This Clift Head is perhaps C. York as it agrees exactly with the lat^d—If so it may be known by the Paps lying at the back of it & a few reddish Sand Hills near it—All the others are white sand

At 2 Little or no wood on the Coast & the North^n land insight tapering to a point with some Hillocks on it—

Apparently in Sound^gs— More see & every thing indicating less sheltered by any Reef to the Es^d/w. A few miles of land now abreast of us looks like Downs with high sloping Clifts to the Sea.—

I brought to for the night being Windy—

Went on shore found signs of the Natives having been here Turtling—Isl^d 1½ Round Rocky all round except a point at the SW End were we lay.—

From the Hillock Point formed a deep Bay & Inlet—Ab^t 6 Miles farther North opposite the Isl^d the land very low & covered with white Sand for 6 Miles farther north, it then gets higher towards P^t Possession or what I take to be such off which lie sev^l Islands the north^ly the highest and to the east of which lie 4 high Rock much like each other.—Wood in most places. but apparently barren in other respects.—Other Isl^ds lie to the NNW of high Isl^d—No Sand Hills—Rocky as I advanced towards the NW the Main in the SW appeared as a Parcel of High Islands which might from the appearance of it be called the Bay of Islands. But I believe the[y] may all join by low land.— More land was now seen ahead. and small Keys to the NW taking that direction as if the Boundary of the Reef was Such—The Country now seems to be Rocky & no Sand Hills

At 11 the Main appeared to be broken & formed deep Inlets & Isl^ds—Isl^ds more considerable than what we have seen & some very high appeared in the N & NW—The whole seemes a wonderfull place—I do not imagine [that?] any of the Isld^s are joined by Reefs, if I may judge from those I've seen and now pass several between me & the Main, & others are constantly appearing.— At Noon discovered a Reef extend^g from West to NE whether this reef joins round to the S^d I cannot say or whether it is connected to some more to the North—Some small Keys, I could just see in the Range of the Reef & therefore perhaps the High Isl^d to the north^d are not connected with it.—

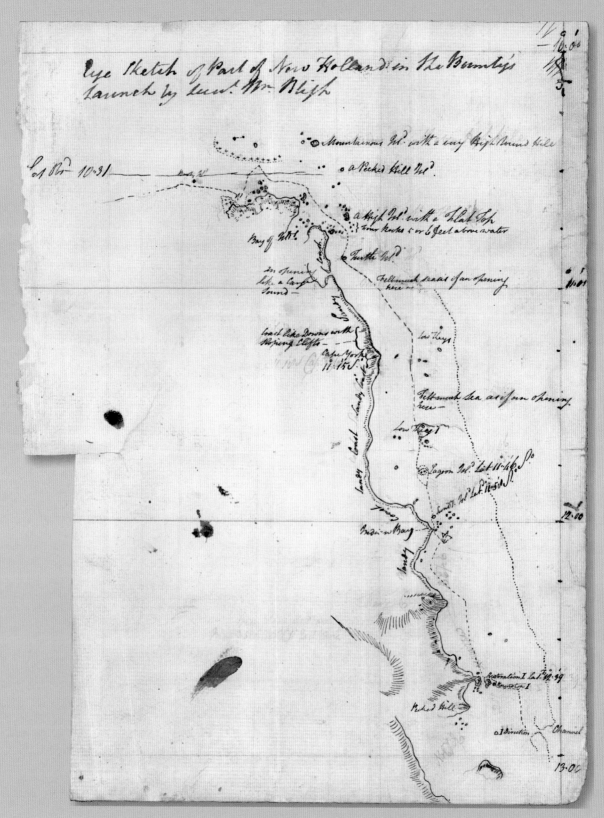

Bligh's notebook sketch of part of the coast of New Holland

On 3 June, Bligh announced to the crew that they would be clear of New Holland that afternoon. As Bligh proceeded up the north-east coast, he concentrated on his surveying, as the weather had become much more conducive to taking accurate sightings and constructing a chart. His dedication to exploring the potential of the coastline for future development was re-ignited. In his *Narrative*, he observes:

> *The coast to the northward and westward of the Bay of Islands had a very different appearance from that to the southward. It was high and woody, with many islands close to it, and had a very broken appearance. Among these islands are fine bays, and convenient places for shipping.*

Bligh's 'Eye Sketch of Part of New Holland' in his notebook appears to be the original from which the map published in his *A Voyage to the South Sea* was produced. In *Narrative*, Bligh states that his chart was not intended to supersede Cook's chart, owing to the difficulties he was experiencing in the open boat. He said that he included it to make his narrative more intelligible, but Bligh was proud of his achievement and thought that he had created a chart with improved accuracy, at least in some areas. Matthew Flinders took a copy of Bligh's chart with him in 1802–1803 when he was surveying the north of New Holland. He was most impressed that the chart did indeed provide more precise drawings of certain sections of the coastline than Cook's version, and he was full of praise for Bligh, writing:

> *To the west of Cape Cornwal, the islands are laid down according to my bearings and observations in the* Investigator *and* Cumberland; *and they have less agreement both in situation and appearance with Captain Cook's Chart, than they have with that made by captain Bligh in the Bounty's launch. It has been a cause of much surprise, that under such distress of hunger and fatigue and of anxiety still greater than these, and whilst running before a strong breeze in an open boat, captain Bligh should have been able to gather materials for a chart; but that this chart should possess a considerable a share of accuracy, is a subject for admiration.*

Steering to the south-west, towards the westernmost part of the land in sight, the launch encountered some large sandbanks that ran from the coast. To avoid them, the men steered

Captain Matthew Flinders used Bligh's chart when surveying New Holland over 10 years after the journey of the *Bounty*'s launch

to the north again and, having rounded them, directed their course to the west. At eight o'clock in the evening, on 4 June, they once more launched into the open ocean. Bligh writes in his published account:

> *Miserable as our situation was in every respect, I was secretly surprised to see that it did not appear to affect any one so strongly as myself; on the contrary, it seemed as if they had embarked on a voyage to Timor, in a vessel sufficiently calculated for safety and convenience ... if any one of them had despaired, he would most probably have died before we reached New Holland.*

Bligh announced that eight or 10 days might bring them to land and set a course to the west south-west to counteract the southerly winds, in case they should blow strong. Once more, the regime of rationing was implemented and supplemented by catching seabirds, the blood being given to the weakest onboard.

Bligh's naturalist's eye was still engaged and he noted a number of water snakes ringed in yellow and black and large quantities of rock weed. Morale onboard was deteriorating as the seas grew rougher and the men became weaker from continuous bailing. Timor still seemed to be a world away and Bligh introduced an even stricter regime of food rationing, fearing that he would miss Timor and need to extend the journey.

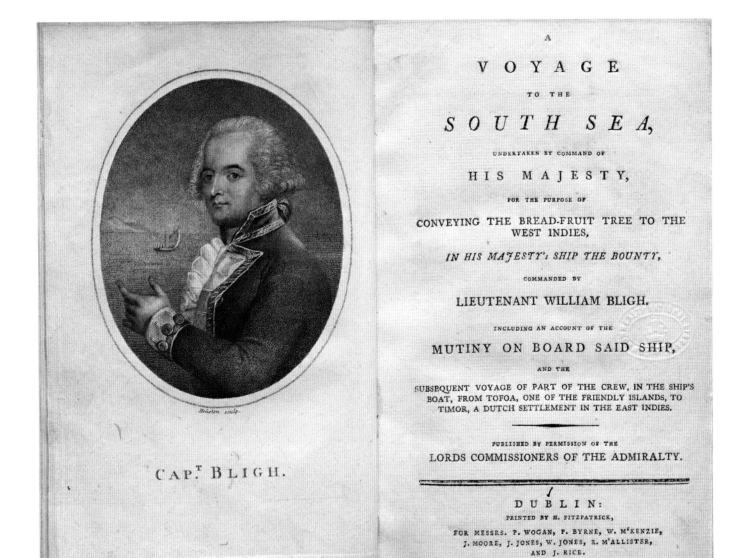

CAP.^T BLIGH.

A

VOYAGE

TO THE

SOUTH SEA,

UNDERTAKEN BY COMMAND OF

HIS MAJESTY,

FOR THE PURPOSE OF

CONVEYING THE BREAD-FRUIT TREE TO THE
WEST INDIES,

IN HIS MAJESTY's SHIP THE BOUNTY,

COMMANDED BY

LIEUTENANT WILLIAM BLIGH.

INCLUDING AN ACCOUNT OF THE

MUTINY ON BOARD SAID SHIP,

AND THE

SUBSEQUENT VOYAGE OF PART OF THE CREW, IN THE SHIP'S
BOAT, FROM TOFOA, ONE OF THE FRIENDLY ISLANDS, TO
TIMOR, A DUTCH SETTLEMENT IN THE EAST INDIES.

PUBLISHED BY PERMISSION OF THE

LORDS COMMISSIONERS OF THE ADMIRALTY.

DUBLIN:

PRINTED BY H. FITZPATRICK,

FOR MESSRS. P. WOGAN, P. BYRNE, W. M^cKENZIE,
J. MOORE, J. JONES, W. JONES, R. M^cALLISTER,
AND J. RICE.

MDCC XCII.

The frontispiece and title page of Bligh's *A Voyage to the South Sea*, 1792

'People very weak ...
no appearance of Land
Desperately seeking Timor

H	K	F	Course	Wind	Remarks
1	4		WbS	SE	Strong Trade & fair Wᵗʳ
2	4				much Sea —
3	3	6			Several Gannets & Bottle
4	4				& tⁱⁱ —
5	4	6		"	We now are anxious to
6	4	4		"	see the land my reck.ᵍ
7	4	2	Rechf up		being nearly up by H. Moore.
8	4	2	WbS —		People very weak. —
9	4	4			Servd Bread & Water for
10	4	6			supper. — No appearance
11	4	4			of Land. —
12	5				
1	5				9.0 — 128.0
2	5				9.41 — 129.50
3	4	4			1.50
4	4	4		SSE	6.50
5	4	4			110 Miles
6	4	4		"	Gannet but no sight of Land
7	4	4		"	
8	4	4		"	Several pieces of Rockweed
9	4				Pleasant Wᵗʳ — Servd Bread
10	3	6			& water —
11	4				
12	3	6		"	Fine Wᵗʳ & Less Sea Very hazy
					No signs Land — Bread & Water
	107		Latᵈ Obˢ 9.41 S 9.24 Dᴿ		

Bad Steerage —

H	K	F	Courses	Wind	Rem^s Thursd^y 11th June 1789
1	4		W½S	SE	Strong Trade & fair W^r
2	4				
3	3	6			Much Sea—
4	4	"			Several Gannets & Boobys & Fish.—
5	4	6	"	"	We now are anxious to see the land my
6	4	4	"	"	reck^g being nearly up by H Moore.
7	4	2	Reck^g up		People very weak.—
8	4	2	WbS		Served Bread & Water for supper.—
9	4	4			no appearance of Land.—
10	4	6			
11	4	4			9.0 — 128.0
12	5	"			9.41 — 129.50
1	5	"			1.50
2	5				60
3	4	4			110 miles
4	4	4		SSE	
5	4	4			
6	4	4	"	"	Gannet but no sigh[t] of Land
7	4	4			
8	4	4	"	"	Several pieces of Rockweed
9	4				Pleasant W^r—Served Bread & Water—
10	3	6			
11	4				
12	3	6	"	"	Fine W^r & Less Sea Very hazy
					no signs Land—Bread & Water

———————

| 107 | | | | Lat Obs | 9° 41'S 9°. 24' DR— |
| | | | | | Distress'd |

Bad steerage—

[Some calculations appear here]

I steered Southerly lest the North part of Timor not being in 9.00' I might from a small error in my course pass it altogether

Any fish, such as flying fish, or seabirds that the men caught were eaten raw

There are small clues in the notebook from 7 June onwards that Bligh was becoming more and more anxious about the condition of his crew, concerned about the accuracy of his calculations (as his own health was deteriorating) and distressed at the sheer physical effort required of everyone to constantly bail the boat in the heavy seas. The weakest of the crew were sustained with teaspoons of wine which he had saved for such an emergency. There were thefts of food and the party was entirely miserable, disputing every possible topic and piece of advice.

Bligh was desperately worried that he might miss Timor. He was using *Tables Requisite*, which had two references, the first to 'Timor (S.W. Point)', which was accurate for latitude and just half a degree too far east for longitude. The second reference for 'Timor Land (S. Point)' was completely inaccurate, referring to the Tanimbar Islands, approximately 240 miles east of the north-east tip of Timor. Bligh's other source book by John Hamilton Moore was even more confusing and inaccurate, as the nine degrees south latitude given for the north end of Timor was 30 minutes too far south. The longitude for Timor is almost two degrees west of that given by Hamilton Moore.

Strangely, the compounding of errors and Bligh's often misguided corrections at this point in the journey resulted in a course free from too many real errors. Bligh 'lost' over two degrees of longitude between Torres Strait and Timor, which more than compensated for the one and a half degrees of westerly error caused by the correction he made to manoeuvre around what he thought was Cape York. On 11 June, when he was acutely anxious about his location, he was actually 30 miles closer to Timor than he thought he was.

Bligh's failing strength and associated mental fatigue is evident in the uncharacteristic error he made when he compared his position of noon 11 June with Hamilton Moore's position for North Timor. He incorrectly labelled the difference of longitude in minutes of arc as miles, but the mistake had little impact on the progress of the launch.

A copy of the front page of Table XX in *Tables Requisite* that Bligh used for his calculations

T A B L E XX

CONTAINING

THE LATITUDES OF PLACES,

WITH

THEIR LONGITUDES FROM THE MERIDIAN OF THE ROYAL OBSERVATORY AT GREENWICH:

ALSO

THE TIME OF HIGH WATER

AT THE

FULL AND CHANGE OF THE MOON,

AT THOSE PLACES WHERE IT IS KNOWN.

An entry in Bligh's
notebook on 12 June
1789, which reads 'Fine
W^r & hazy anxiously
hope for Timor.—Very
weak & distressed'

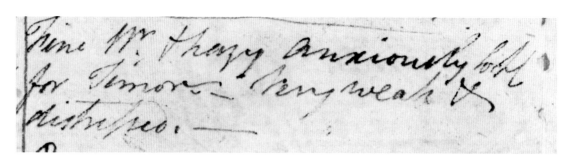

Bligh could see from the traces of rock weed drifting past and from the increasing numbers of seabirds that he was close to land, but the worsening condition of the men around him caused him to write about their appearance:

> *An extreme weakness, swelled legs, hollow and ghastly countenances, great propensity to sleep and an apparent debility of understanding, give me melancholy proofs of an approaching dissolution of some of my people.*

This was Bligh's darkest hour. He stood to lose everything if he did not find the coast of Timor. The loss of the *Bounty* was a disaster but, if his navigational skills and stubborn will failed to rescue the loyalists and deliver his surveys, notes and logs to the authorities, then his failure amounted to total disgrace. One word conveys more emotion than any other entry in the logbook because it is so uncharacteristically negative. The word 'Distress'd' is entered on 11 June under the notation, 'Lat Obs 9° 41' S 9° 24' DR'.

Bligh was at his wit's end, ill from the oily part of a fish's stomach he had eaten; watching his men decline rapidly, he must have been praying very hard for a miracle to happen. Fortunately it did.

ATTAGEN ARIEL. *Gould.*

Small Frigate Bird.

In his notebook, Bligh noted the presence of man-o'-war birds (frigatebirds)

'At Day Break Timor'
Reaching Timor

5	4		West	Many Gulls toward Breed
6	4			& steer for Wipper
7	4	4	East	No appearance of Land
8	4	6		Caught a Booby by hand
9	5			At 3 saw Timor NbNW to WbN
10	5	4	24 Days May	
11	4	4	12 / 41	At Day break Timor NbE½N
12	5			7 leags. to SWbS low land 2 leags.
				Bore away. —
1	5			
2	5			At 7 land opened with the low
3	4	6		land at SW
4	3		NbE	At 8 the extremes of Timor from
5	3			SWbW 5 leags. to NbEN 6 leags. &
6	3		NbE	Pt. of low land set at day break NbW
7	3		SW	3 Miles —

At Day Light I fetched within with Low land
which formed the SE. part of the Isd. — It was
woody near the shore & other parts bear. An
Opening like a Harbour appeared very West abt.
5 Miles to the NW of which appeared a cultivated country & from the arrangement of
the Trees on one part it looked like a Gentlemans
Seat. A great sea sat on the shore & were only 5
Miles from it I therefore hauled out for a Wind
to clear the SE. Pt. 2 leags. — I would have
put into this

H	K	F	Courses	Winds	Remarks
5	4		West	"	Many Gulls Served Bread & water for
6	4		"	"	supper
7	4	4		East	no appearance of Land
8	4	6			Caught a Booby by hand
9	5				At 3 Saw Timor WNW to WSW
10	5		29 Days May		
11	4	4	12		At Day Break Timor NE½N 7 leags to
12	5		41		SWbS low land 2 leag.
1	5				Bore away.—
2	5				
3	4	6			At 7 Land opened with the low land at SW
4	3		NNE	"	At 8 the extremes of Timor from SWbW
5	3				5 leags to NEbN 6 leags & Pt of low land
6	3	"	SbE	EbS	set at day break NbW 3 Miles—

At Day Light I fetched in with lowland which formed the SEn part of the Isld—
It was woody near the shore & other parts bear. An Opening like a Harbour
appeared bearg West abt 5 Miles to the NW of which appeared a cultivated
Country & from the arrangement of the Trees on one part it looked like a
Gentlemans Seat. A Great sea sat on the Shore & were only 5 Miles from it I
therefore hauled out on a Wind to clear the SEn Pt abt 2 leags—I would have
put into this apparent Port but I feared it might be difficult for me to get
out again.
Interior parts Mountainous & Woody
Appeared the mouth of a River at the point of lowland—10h
Mountains pleasantly diversified by cleared Spots wch we take to be
cultivated. See no Houses or Smokes. The Extrems We now see are high but
the shore has been low we have passed hitherto—Plenty of wood. I intended
to have gone on the South Side but I could not get round & I expect the
Govern residence on the SW part.

View of Coupang, Timor (detail of image on pages 168–169)

Bligh's first entry in his notebook for Friday 12 June reports that the weather was fine and hazy and that the men were anxiously hoping to sight Timor. They were distraught and very weak. Many gulls were noted and, at last, at 3 o'clock in the afternoon, they saw the coast of Timor. At daylight the next day, Bligh sailed closer and described 'lowland … woody near the shore & other parts bear'. Still Bligh feared to enter a port out of which he did not know how to navigate, and his primary objective was to find the Dutch settlement, wherever that might be.

Timor is the largest and most eastern island of the Nusa Tenggara Islands stretching south-west to north-east. It is roughly 300 miles long (480 kilometres), it has a maximum width of 66 miles (105 kilometres) and the topography is mountainous, intersected by deep valleys. There are resemblances with the climate and vegetation of northern Australia. The forests of sandalwood were the strongest attraction for foreigners, and there is evidence to suggest that sandalwood trading took place there from the seventh century AD.

In 1566, Portuguese Dominican Friars settled in the neighbouring island of Solor and a settlement sprang up composed of Portuguese soldiers, their indigenous wives and their children (a mixed race known as Topasses) and indigenous people who had converted. In 1613, the Dutch reached Timor and met with a favourable reception from the lord or kupand, ruler of Helong, but they did not stay. In 1653, they transferred their garrison from Solor to Coupang and this remained the Dutch cultural centre in Timor until Indonesia's independence. By the seventeenth century, the Dutch had supplanted the Portuguese in South-East Asia, with the exception of Solor, Flores and Timor. The Dutch tried desperately to take over the sandalwood trade from the Portuguese but could not unravel the elaborate Portuguese trade networks that were largely based on the activities of the Dominican missionaries, who organised opposition to the Dutch. In 1769, the Portuguese governor abandoned Lifao, in Timor, to rebels, evacuating the inhabitants to Dili, the new capital. Meanwhile, the Dutch concentrated on developing Coupang into the main port of Timor. By the end of the eighteenth century, the Dutch only remained in Timor because of the loss of prestige that they would suffer if they admitted that the Portuguese held the monopoly in sandalwood trading. Luckily for Bligh, the Dutch had maintained an impressive, hospitable and gracious presence through their governor.

In *Narrative*, Bligh describes with joy and pride the moment the launch party sighted land:

> *It is not possible for me to describe the pleasure which the blessing of the sight of land diffused among us. It appeared scarce credible, that in an open boat, and so poorly*

TIMOR.

Vue de la rade, de la ville et du fort hollandois de Coupang.

View of Coupang, Timor

provided, we should have been able to reach the coast of Timor in forty-one days after leaving Tofoa, having in that time run, by our log, a distance of 3618 miles, and that, notwithstanding our extreme distress, no one should have perished in the voyage.

Bligh did not know where the Dutch settlement was located but, following his intuition, he bore towards the south-west part of the island. Although they must all have been in a fever of anticipation, if there had been any impatient remarks from the crew, Bligh makes no mention of them. Instead, he relates the general mood of interest in the passing landscape:

We were greatly delighted with the general look of the country, which exhibited many cultivated spots and beautiful situations; but we could only see a few small huts, whence I concluded no European resided in this part of the island. Much sea ran towards the shore, so that landing with a boat was impracticable.

The men were forced to dine once more on bread and booby caught the night before, Bligh giving wine to the two worst afflicted men. The journey in the launch continued and there was a change in the landscape:

During the afternoon, we continued our course along a low woody shore, with innumerable palm-trees, called the Fan Palm, from the leaf spreading like a fan; but we had now lost all signs of cultivation, and the country had not so fine an appearance as it had to the eastward.

Bligh was anxious lest they pass the Dutch settlement at night and miss the entrance, so he anchored the launch about half a league from the shore, and served bread and water for supper. Waking at two in the morning, Bligh realised they had drifted during the night and set about returning to follow the shore, discovering that they were near the island of Roti. Reaching the shore they had left, Bligh anchored in a sandy bay to more carefully find his bearings. At this point, he notes that the master and carpenter wished to leave the boat and look for supplies but, when no-one would accompany them, they abandoned the plan. Perhaps the men feared that the slightest hint of insubordination would send Bligh over the edge of reason irredeemably and that he would run them through before they could reach safety.

Finally, in the afternoon, the launch was able to turn towards the shore for a safe landing place near friendly inhabitants:

At two o'clock this afternoon, having run through a very dangerous breaking sea, the cause of which I attributed to a strong tide setting to windward, and shoal water, we discovered a spacious bay or sound, with a fair entrance about two or three miles wide. I now conceived hopes that our voyage would be soon at an end, as no place could appear more eligible for shipping, or more likely to be chosen for an European settlement; I therefore came to a grapnel near the east side of the entrance, in a small sandy bay, where we saw a hut, a dog, and some cattle: and I immediately sent the boatswain and gunner away to the hut, to discover the inhabitants.

While his men went ashore, Bligh remained active on the launch, noticing both the position of a reef just off shore that would be covered at high tide (and therefore be dangerous) and a deep channel suitable for the entry of an armed ship. For a naval commander, this kind of information could have many valuable uses in the future.

The boatswain and gunner returned with 'five Indians', who Bligh described as being of a dark tawny colour, with long black hair, and who chewed a lot of betel. Their dress was minimal—a piece of cloth around the hips with a knife held in the folds. A scarf was wrapped around the head and another draped from the shoulders, functioning as a bag to hold the betel. They brought the crew pieces of dried turtle and some ears of Indian corn. Bligh had discovered that the governor resided at Coupang, 'some distance to the NE', and he engaged one of the local inhabitants as a pilot to lead the party. Once more, the crew was forced to spend another night on the launch, sleeping within a short distance of the channel leading to Coupang:

We kept close to the shore, and continued rowing till four o'clock, when I brought to a grapnel, and gave another allowance of bread and wine to all hands. As soon as we had rested a little, we weighed again, and rowed till near day-light, when I came to a grapnel, off a small fort and town, which the pilot told me was Coupang.

THE GANNET.

Having Timor in their sights but not yet able to land, Bligh and his men once again had to endure a meal of bread and raw seabird meat

'All hands overjoyed & in
the greatest spirits'
Landfall

Reml

A most charming extensive Bay 2
Miles or more across the Entrance and
considerably more extensive to the North
and Eastward. — Md lye at. 5 leagt SSW
The coast lies East and
West without. — Whether the Nth. off it
it is Rotto & Savu I am at a loss to
know & I have no Books to tell me
& my recollection to be

The land makes in the Bay with mod.
risings joined by lower grounds —
Saw a Dog & some Cattle on our shore
Mr. Peckover & Cole I sent after them.

In Rounding the Bay, the coast to this place
along shore where
the land is low it appeared shoal water
& broke in high Seas. —

About 4 Party returned with some Malays
one of whom agreed to go with me to Compon
wch I understood was the Governors residence,
by shewing him a parcel of Dollars. —

All hands overjoyed & in the greatest spirits
at this happy appearance of an end to our
distress — Got a few heads of Indian Corn —

14 June 1789 ——

9   Hoisted a Small Jack we made, in the

10   M. Shrouds as in distress—At 6 I had to

11   leave to come on Shore.—

12   At 9 All hands came on shore

       At Noon—Boat hauled into the River & every thing out—

Rem^s
—————
A most charming extensive Bay 2 Miles or more across the Entrance and
considerably more extensive to the North^d and Eastward.—Isl^{ds} lye ab^t
5 leag^s SSW
The Coast lies East and West without.—Whether the Isld^s off it it is Rotto
[=Roti] & Savu I am at a loss to know & I have no Books to tell me & my
recollection so bad—
The Land makes in the Bay with mod risings joined by lower Grounds—
Saw a Dog & some Cattle on our Shore
Mrs Peckover & Cole I sent after them.
—————————

In Rounding the Bay, along shore the Coast to this place where the land is low
it appeared shoalwater & broke in high seas.—
————————

About 4 Party returned with some Melays one of whom agreed to go with me
to Coupang wch I understood was the Governors residence, by showing him a
parcel of Dollars.—
All hands overjoyed & in the greatest spirits at this happy appearance of an
end to our distress—Got a few heads of Indian Corn—& some dryed pieces
of callypees of Turtle [calipee=cartilage cut from among the bones of the
bottom shell].
I might perhaps have got some trifles else but as it was clear to me that such
an elligible Place for Shipping would have some settlement I relyed on the
Mellay & went on.—
————————

The Party found a family or two of Mellays—The Women curtseyed & all
shewed every sign of having connection with Europeans.—
————————

We kept the Eastern side of the bay on board to the NE & ENE—making a true NEbE course nearly I believe dist about 8 Miles to were we [anchor symbol] at 10 PM. The Sea was here open to the North^d & NW & I found I was here at the north Entrance of this Spacious Harbour 1½ across. While I lay in the South entrance the Ebb Tide run from the North^d & before I left it showed me a reef about 2 Cables length from the East shore where I was which seemed to run in the direction of the shore of this side of the entrance.—A Ship must therefore carefully attend to it, as they will see nothing of it at high Water.—

Near the Shores is a flat of shoal water but farther off plenty of depth I have no doubt for any Ships.—

In the Middle of this North entrance I sounded 10 fm^s. no ground

At 1 In the morn^g we rowed along shore (after making some fruitless attempts with the sails) to the Eastward ENE ab^t 5 miles

Saw some Vessels in the Road [=a sheltered stretch of water outside a harbour where ships can anchor] wch gave us most inexpressable pleasure. And a little before day I came to a Grapnel off a Small Town & Fort wch the Pilot told me was Coupang.—

At day break I was desired to come on shore by a Soldier who was sent down to the beach & who conducted me to the Fort, but found no person of consequence & the Governor they told me could not be spoke wth untill 10 O'Clock in the morn^g.—

Met an English Sailor who belonged to the large Ship in the Road He conducted me to his Captain—Called Spikerman.—This Gentleman behaved with great goodness, & after having told him of my situation I requested care & a situation for my People & officers might be prepared without delay.—

He therefore gave the necessary orders for their accomodation & victualling for the present but more could not be done untill the Governor who was Ill, permitted any one to visit him.—

The *Pandora* saga

The mutiny on the *Bounty* was an affront to the Crown and it was essential that the mutineers be hunted down and returned to England to face justice. There were, however, many pressing concerns for the Admiralty at this time, not least the threat of war with Spain over possession of the permanent settlement of Nootka in Canada, a strategic position controlling access to the north-west passage between the Atlantic and the Pacific.

As first-class ships were required for the more serious threats of naval battles, the ship taken out of mothballs to chase the mutineers was the sixth-rate frigate of 24 guns, the *Pandora*. Launched in 1779, she had been moored at Chatham since September 1783. Edwards was appointed commander on the recommendation of Lord Ducie. The vessel was crammed with provisions for the 12-month voyage and also carried a complete set of stores for the *Bounty*, so that she could be sailed back to England. The crew was faced with exceptionally cramped conditions. The ship's surgeon, George Hamilton, writes:

> *What rendered our situation still more distressing, was the crowded state of the ship being filled to the hatchways with stores and provisions, for, like weevils, we had to eat a hole in our bread, before we had a place to lay down in; every officer's cabin, the Captain's not excepted, being filled with provisions and stores.*

On 7 November 1790, the *Pandora* left England heading for Tenerife. Before she sailed, she received onboard as third lieutenant, Thomas Hayward, who had served as midshipman on the *Bounty*, a man who received little respect from the crew while serving under Bligh. He proved himself violent and vindictive towards the mutineers when they were located, although he knew full well that some of the men had gone with Christian only because there was no room in the launch. Two young men, Thomas Ellison and Peter Heywood, could not have been held responsible for the fact that they had ended up with Christian in the confusion of the mutiny and, through misunderstandings and the chaos of Bligh's removal, there were plausible reasons why a good number of the crew sailed with Christian.

In Rio de Janeiro, Hamilton recorded that the voyage had purposes other than just the arrest of the mutineers, describing the 'unremitting zeal' of lieutenants Robert Corner and Thomas Hayward 'in procuring and nursing such plants as might be useful at Otaheiti or the Islands we might discover'.

Edwards logged three new islands as he entered the Pacific, naming the first Ducie's Island, after his patron. He then dropped anchor in Matavai Bay on the north coast of Tahiti on the morning of 23 March. An indigenous man came onboard the ship and told Edwards that several of the mutineers were on the island, but that Christian and some followers had left. Soon after this, Joseph Coleman, the armourer, who was not a true mutineer, came onboard. He, Charles Norman and Thomas McIntosh had tried to get into the launch with Bligh but had been prevented by Christian, and Bligh had recorded his belief in their innocence. Coleman told Edwards of the fate of the mutineers. Sixteen had left the *Bounty* at Tahiti and two of these, Charles Churchill and Matthew Thompson, were dead. These men had lived with a chief in a remote part of the island. Churchill had become an esteemed friend of the chief and, on the chief's death, he had taken on the role of district chief. Thompson had killed him in a jealous rage.

Next to come onboard was Heywood, 17 at the time of the mutiny, and George Stewart. Both men were of good families. Edwards had no interest in talking to the men to ascertain who was truly mutinous. They were all clapped in irons and confined below decks, isolated from their friends on the island, awaiting the building of a prison on the quarterdeck which came to be known as 'Pandora's Box'. Later that afternoon, Richard Skinner, master's servant and barber on the *Bounty* surrendered and next day, the blind fiddler, Michael Byrn, arrived.

James Morrison, Norman and Ellison, who had made a hasty attempt to escape in a schooner they had built under Morrison's guidance, thought better of it and returned to be locked up. Edwards sent two boats with armed crews to bring back other men who had fled into hiding. On 9 April, they returned with Henry Hilbrant and McIntosh. The next day, Thomas Burkitt, John Millward, John Sumner and William Muspratt returned on the second boat. Fourteen mutineers had been apprehended, two were dead and there were just eight more at large. The crew of the *Pandora* remained at Tahiti for 47 days, then left to search for Christian.

After four months investigating the Pacific islands most likely to have been reached by Christian, Edwards found no trace of the remaining mutineers and decided that he must end the search if he was to get through the Endeavour Straits, as it was already late in the season and the north-westerly monsoons were threatening. His list of achievements at this point was commendable. He had captured most of the mutineers, he had collected breadfruit, other plants and curiosities from the indigenous peoples he had encountered and he had searched thoroughly for Christian.

List of illustrations

Editor's notes: Pages from William Bligh's notebook and the list of mutineers, MS 5393, Manuscripts Collection, appear throughout the book. Both items can be viewed at http://nla.gov.au/nla.ms-ms5393.

Page 2 image: Rare and fragile material must be handled with care to avoid accidental damage. This may involve the use of cotton or nitrile gloves, or freshly washed bare hands. Library staff take advice from expert conservators about which method to use when handling specific items, and the image on page 2 shows a Library staff member handling the notebook with scrupulously cleaned hands. Members of the public are required to wear gloves for handling some Library material.

Endpapers
Thomas Conder (active 1775–1801)
A New & Accurate Chart of the Discoveries of Captn Cook & Other Later Circumnavigators: Exhibiting the Whole Coast of New South Wales ... (detail) 1794?
coloured map; 41.0 x 32.8 cm
Maps Collection, nla.map-rm514

Page iv
Ebenezer Edward Gostelow (1866–1944)
Four Species of Gannet (detail) 1940
watercolour; 50.7 x 63.5 cm
Pictures Collection, nla.pic-an3904724

Page 4
Logline
Courtesy Australian National Maritime Museum

Page 6
Richard Earlom (engraver, 1743–1822);
Johann Zoffany (artist, 1733–1810)
Their Most Sacred Majesties George the IIId and Queen Charlotte 1771
mezzotint; 50.3 x 58.5 cm
Pictures Collection, nla.pic-an9576659

Page 8
Unknown artist (possibly Sydney Parkinson (1745?–1771))
Bread Fruit 1769?
watercolour; 31.0 x 38.5 cm
Pictures Collection, nla.pic-an6243457

Page 9 (left)
Thomas Gosse (1765–1844)
Transplanting of the Bread Fruit Trees from Otaheite 1796
hand-coloured mezzotint; 52.4 x 60.6 cm
Pictures Collection, nla.pic-an6016209

Page 9 (right)
John Frederick Miller (active 1768–1780)
A Branch of the Bread-fruit Tree with the Fruit 1773
engraving; 36.9 x 30.4 cm
plate 11 reproduced from *An Account of the Voyages Undertaken by the Order of His Present Majesty, for Making Discoveries in the Southern Hemisphere*, vol. 2, by John Hawkesworth (London, 1773)
Pictures Collection, nla.pic-an9184914

Page 11
Geoffrey Chapman Ingleton (1908–1998)
Bounty 1937
sepia etching; 22.5 x 28.8 cm
Pictures Collection, nla.pic-an6152178
Courtesy Kelly King

Page 12
Attributed to John Webber (1751–1793)
Bligh as a Young Midshipman in the 1770s
oil on canvas; 62.2 x 74.3 cm
reproduced from *William Bligh, Extraordinary Seaman: A Look at His Life and Times: An Exhibition Held by the Earl and Countess of Devon in Their Home during Maritime England Year 1982*
compiled by Stephen Walters
(London: Pitcairn Press, 1982)

Page 13
Unknown artist
Captain Cook's Interview with Natives in Adventure Bay, Van Dieman's Land, 29 January 1777 2003
b&w reproduction; 33.7 x 49.4 cm
Maps Collection, nla.map-nk10592a-9

Page 15
John Webber (1751–1793)
Elizabeth Bligh née Betham 1782
oil on canvas; 61.0 x 71.1 cm
reproduced from *William Bligh, Extraordinary Seaman: A Look at His Life and Times: An Exhibition Held by the Earl and Countess of Devon in Their Home during Maritime England Year 1982*
compiled by Stephen Walters
(London: Pitcairn Press, 1982)

Page 20
Inigo Barlow (engraver); W. Collings (artist)
The Pirates Seizing Captn. Bligh 1790s
engraving; 13.5 x 8.7 cm
Pictures Collection, nla.pic-an9454400

Page 21
Antoine Cardon (engraver, 1772–1813); William Evans (artist, active 1800–1822)
The Right Hon. Sir Joseph Banks, Bart., K.B. 1810
hand-coloured stipple engraving; 38.5 x 30.2 cm
Pictures Collection, nla.pic-an6053449

Page 22 (top)
Jo Hykin
William Bligh's tombstone, St Mary's, Lambeth, London, 2009
colour photograph
Courtesy Dr Jo Hykin

Page 22 (bottom)
Great Britain Hydrographic Department, engraved by Davies &
Company
*South Pacific Ocean, Society Islands, Tahiti and Moorea (Otaheit'e
and Eimeo)* 1880
2 maps on 1 sheet; 95.3 x 60.3 cm
Maps Collection, nla.map-rm1681

Page 24
Charles Beyer (1792–?)
John Adams 1830s
etching; 9.5 x 12.0 cm
Pictures Collection, nla.pic-an9281376

Page 27
Louis Choris (1795–1828)
Fruit du Cocotier 1822
Plate 70 reproduced from *Voyage pittoresque autour du monde ...*
by Louis Choris (Paris: Imprimerie de Firmin Didot, 1821–1822)
hand-coloured lithograph; 25.3 x 41.0 cm
Pictures Collection, nla.pic-an10465542

Page 28
Unknown artist
The Cocoa-nut Tree
reproduced from *Dangerous Voyage of Captain Bligh in an Open
Boat over 1200 Leagues of the Ocean, in the Year 1789* by William
Bligh (London: John Arliss, 1818)

Page 34
Robert Dodd (1748–1816)
*The Mutineers Turning Lieut. Bligh and Part of the Officers and Crew
Adrift from His Majesty's Ship the* Bounty 1790
hand-coloured aquatint; 46.8 x 62.5 cm
Pictures Collection, nla.pic-an6308155

Page 37
Doug Sim
St Bees School foundation block from the church tower
(Whitehaven, Cumbria)
This work is licensed under the CC Attribution-ShareAlike 3.0
Unported licence

Page 40
Conway Shipley (1824–?)
Bounty Bay, Pitcairn Island 1851
hand-coloured lithograph; 20.3 x 27.3 cm
Pictures Collection, nla.pic-an9058533

Page 43
John Webber (1752–1793)
A View in Matavai, Otaheite 1787
hand-coloured aquatint; 29.3 x 43.0 cm
Pictures Collection, nla.pic-an7678387

Page 48
Robert Dodd (1748–1816)
*The Mutineers Turning Lieut. Bligh and Part of the Officers and Crew
Adrift from His Majesty's Ship the* Bounty (detail) 1790
hand-coloured aquatint; 46.8 x 62.5 cm
Pictures Collection, nla.pic-an6308155

Page 49
See caption for page iv above

Page 51
Edwin Augustus Porcher (1878–?)
*Australia, Booby Island in Torres Straits Where a Post Office Was
Erected* 1843
watercolour; 12.2 x 25.3 cm
Pictures Collection, nla.pic-an4102934

Page 56
Robert Cleveley (1747–1809)
*The Attempt by Capt. Bligh of the Bounty Who with 18 Sailors Had
Been Set Adrift in an Open Boat on April 28th, 1789, to Land on
Tofoa Island* 1790
watercolour; 50.7 x 63.5 cm
Pictures Collection, nla.pic-an6489811

Page 59
William Hodges (1744–1797)
View from Point Venus, Island of Otaheite 1774
oil on canvas; 29.2 x 39.4 cm
Pictures Collection, nla.pic-an2288476

Page 60
George Tobin (1768–1838)
Point Venus, Island of Otaheite 1792
watercolour; 15.1 x 24.1 cm
Pictures Collection, nla.pic-an2970399

Page 66
A copy of the draught from which the *Bounty's* launch was built
reproduced from *The Bligh Notebook: Rough Account—Lieutenant
Wm Bligh's Voyage in the* Bounty's *Launch from the Ship to Tofua
and from Thence to Timor 28 April to 14 June 1789 with a Draft List
of the* Bounty *Mutineers* by John Bach (Canberra: National Library
of Australia, 1986)

Page 68
Don McIntyre on the Talisker Bounty Boat Expedition arriving at
Restoration Island, 2010
colour photograph
Courtesy Don McIntyre

I now ordered everyone to come on shore which is as much as some of them could being so weak as to be scarce able to walk.—Among these were the Surgeon Mr Ledward, who was reduced to meer skin & bones and Lawrence Lebogue a Seaman equally as bad—Those would certainly have died in a few days—Sevral others were getting ill through a want of resolution and spirits, and all in a very weak condition & scarce able to walk & support themselves. I ranked Among the few of the heartyest ones & was certainly the strongest on my Legs but reduced like the others very much & it was favorable to all as I was able to move about & procure the necessary wants.—

At 11 O'Clock I was introduced to the Resident or Governor Wm Adriaan Van Este whose title here is—Koopman en Operhoisd tot Coepang op het Eyland groot Timor.—This Gentleman shewed himself possessed of every feeling of a humane & good man, he received me with great affection ordered refreshments to be got & a House to be cleared for my use, but under this Roof I was obliged to take seamen & Officers or send them to the Hospital or on board of C. Spikⁿ Ship—That this might not be the case I divided the small appartments allotted to me as follows—

one Room I gave to the Master Mr Nelson & Mr Peckover the Gunner & Doctor—another or kind of Loft to the other Officers—Another to the Men, and one I took to myself—a Hall was common to all the officers with a good Piazza round the House & the back part was for the use of the Men.—Surgeon came to Visit us—Clothes given—Dinner at Noon.—Mr Nelson Peckover, Mr Samuels & Hayward only would have lived to have got to Batavia.—

The Governor of Timor welcoming Bligh and his men

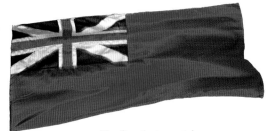

The flag that was taken on a re-enactment of the launch's voyage in 1983

ven at this extremely emotional moment when rescue and sanctuary in a hospitable European residence was so close, Bligh's uppermost thought was how to proceed into the foreign port, observing the correct naval protocols. In Bligh's notebook, above calculations based on his sightings at noon for 7, 9, 11, 13 and 18 May, sketches show his attempts to reproduce the correct pattern on the Great Union flag of England and Scotland. This flag was introduced by James I for use at sea and, in 1634, Charles I decreed that it should be used solely by the Royal Navy. The sketches were used by Bligh to sew the correct flag that would allow him to enter Coupang Harbour in observance of international naval codes. He explains his actions in detail in his *Narrative*:

> *Among the things which the boatswain had thrown into the boat before we left the ship, was a bundle of signal flags that had been made for the boats to show the depth of water in sounding; with these I had, in the course of the passage made a small jack, which I now hoisted in the main shrouds, as a signal of distress; for I did not choose to land without leave.*

Formality and discipline would always define Bligh's actions.

A soldier hailed Bligh to land shortly after daybreak, which he did amidst the interested attentions of many of the local residents. To Bligh's pleasant surprise, he was approached by an English sailor, whose captain was well regarded by the Dutch and, as the governor was ill and unable to meet Bligh, Bligh was invited to meet Captain Spikerman. The captain immediately arranged for Bligh and his men to be received at his own house, while he went in person to the governor to arrange a meeting for Bligh as a matter of urgency. The greatly weakened crew was helped ashore and then to the captain's house where, Bligh noted with pleasure in the logbook, they had 'Tea with Bread and Butter for their Breakfasts'. By the time Bligh wrote

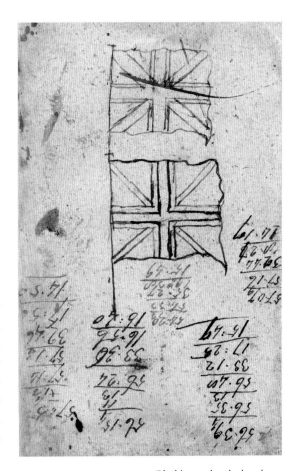

Bligh's notebook sketches of the Great Union flag of England and Scotland, introduced by James I for use at sea

A scene in Coupang

up the story of the launch voyage for publication, he had come to see the black humour in how the starving party must have appeared to the residents of Coupang:

> *An indifferent spectator would have been at a loss which most to admire; the eyes of famine sparkling at immediate relief, or the horror of their preservers at the sight of so many spectres, whose ghastly countenances, if the cause had been unknown, would rather have excited terror than pity. Our bodies were nothing but skin and bones, our limbs were full of sores, and we were cloathed in rags; in this condition, with the tears*

of joy and gratitude flowing down our cheeks, the people of Timor beheld us with a mixture of horror, surprise, and pity.

Although seriously ill himself, the governor, William Adrian Van Este, saw Bligh before the official appointment. He provided a house for Bligh and arranged for the crew to be fed from his own house. At Captain Spikerman's house, the men had washed and had their sores, wounds and injuries attended to by a surgeon. Clothes had been given to them to replace their rags.

Bligh took possession of the house and, foolishly perhaps, decided that his residence should accommodate all the men. Even though he kept a private room for himself, the ill will that had plagued the entire adventure was quick to surface. Once again, Bligh had blurred the boundaries between the status he demanded as commander and the ideal of himself as a father figure liked by his crew. He could not see that, to preserve proper detachment, he needed to maintain a distance from the men.

Bligh provided the governor's second-in-command with the story of their adventures and received permission to send instructions to all Dutch settlements to stop the *Bounty* if she appeared there. He also gained permission for the botanist, David Nelson, with whom Bligh had a genuine friendship, to investigate the country for plant specimens. Alas, Nelson, who always supported Bligh and who the commander thought of as an intellectual equal, never recovered from the effects of the voyage and died not long after they reached Coupang. For Bligh this was a truly bitter blow as the botanist understood, as the others did not, Bligh's passion for natural history observation and his care in making navigation calculations to create a scientific record of the voyage. Nelson would have represented Bligh's efforts to the Admiralty with intelligence and enthusiasm but, more than this, he would have perhaps been the one crew member with whom Bligh could have discussed the ordeal and felt that he was understood. In *Narrative*, Bligh publicly acknowledges his respect for Nelson and includes a detailed description of the funeral ceremony:

July 21st. This day I was employed attending the funeral of Mr. Nelson. The corpse was carried by twelve soldiers drest in black, preceded by the minister; next followed myself and the second governor; then ten gentlemen of the town and the officers of the ships in the harbour; and after them my own officers and people. After reading our burial service, the body was interred behind the chapel, in the burying ground appropriated to the Europeans of the town. I was sorry I could get no tombstone to place over his remains.

From Coupang, Bligh was able to send his first written accounts of the mutiny and what followed to his wife, the Admiralty and his friends. His letter of 19 August to his wife, Betsy, shows Bligh's priorities—fear of dishonour, hope for the future, money safeguarded ('my pursing books') and, finally, affectionate wishes to his children. The 'Dear little stranger' turned out to be twins, born 11 May and christened Frances and Jane:

I know how shocked you will be at this affair but I request of you My Dear Betsy to think nothing of it all is now past & we will again looked forward to future happyness. Nothing but true consciousness as an Officer that I have done well could support me. I cannot write to Your Uncle or anyone, but my publick letters, therefore tell them all that they will find my character respectable & honor untarnished. I have saved my pursing Books so that all my profits hitherto will take place and all will be well. Give my blessing to my Dear Harriet, my Dear Mary, my Dear Betsy & to my Dear little stranger & tell them I shall soon be home.

Bligh found that it was impossible to forget the strain of the last few months as he recuperated in Coupang. He went over and over the events that had led to the mutiny and still he could not really understand what had gone wrong. There was still the long journey home to arrange and, beyond that, Bligh was determined that there would be more voyages and a completion of the duty to his patron, Joseph Banks.

First, however, Bligh had to reach Batavia to find a vessel suitable to take him home before it was too late to catch the Royal Navy fleet, which was departing in October. He purchased a small schooner: 34-feet long for '1000 rix-dollars, and fitted her for sea, under the name of His Majesty's schooner *Resource*'. On 20 August, he left Coupang, where the governor lay at the point of death.

Bligh arrived in Batavia on 1 October and was immediately seized by a fever. He was carried to the countryside and nursed in the physician-general's house under orders from the governor. It was deemed urgent for Bligh to sail given his deteriorating health, but it was not possible to provide a vessel for all the launch party. Bligh and two others embarked on the *Vlydt*, which sailed on 16 October. By 16 December, he was at the Cape of Good Hope and his health was improving. On 14 March, Bligh 'landed at Portsmouth by an Isle of Wight boat'. What thoughts occupied his mind as he stepped ashore in England, not as the triumphant expedition leader but as a commander in an ambiguous position facing a court martial?

The interior of a Timorese house in Coupang

The aftermath

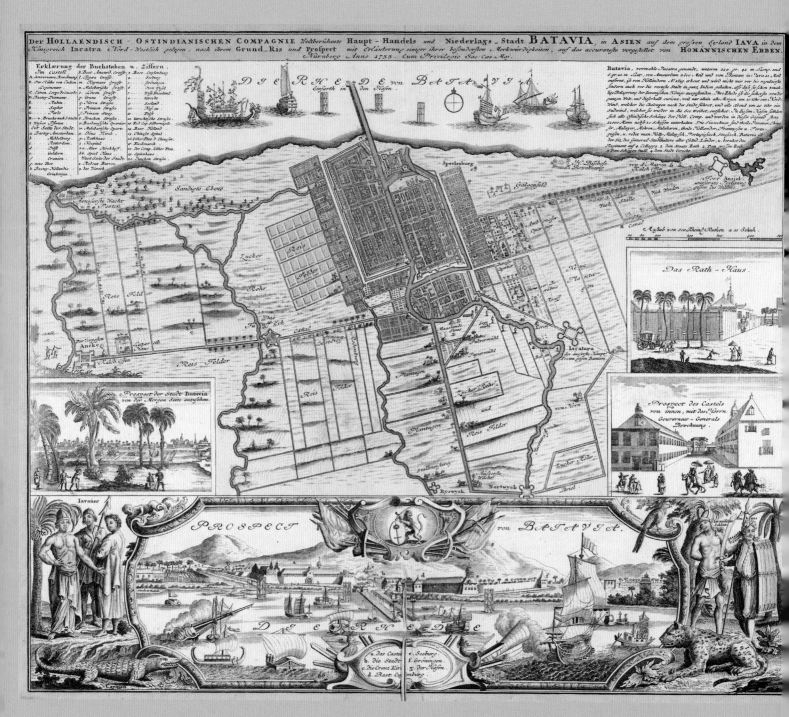

A map showing Dutch East India Company buildings, rice fields, canals and views of Batavia, 1762

The loyalists

What became of the 16 loyal seamen who reached Batavia with Bligh on the *Resource*? At Bligh's request, John Smith and John Samuel accompanied the lieutenant on the *Vlydt*, taking up the only three existing spaces. For those remaining, the Dutch authorities agreed to organise their passage as soon as there was room available on ships. Of the 14 left behind in Batavia, nine arrived safely back in England but five did not survive. Thomas Hall, Peter Linkletter and William Elphinstone died soon after reaching the Dutch East Indies; Robert Lamb died on the journey home; and the ship on which Thomas Ledward had embarked was lost at sea.

For five of the loyalists who had returned to England, their association with Bligh was not over. Smith and Lawrence Lebogue sailed to Tahiti in the *Providence* with Bligh on the second breadfruit expedition in 1791. John Fryer, Robert Tinkler and Bligh all served at the Battle of Copenhagen in 1801 when the British fleet under Nelson's command had a victorious engagement with a Norwegian–Danish fleet. Tinkler was promoted to post-captain and Fryer served as master until 1812. John Samuel remained in the Royal Navy and rose to the rank of paymaster.

Bligh's arrival in London

On his arrival in England, Bligh faced a mandatory court martial for losing his ship. The rest of his surviving *Bounty* launch crew returned from Batavia to be present at the trial. While public opinion was fiercely divided about who was to blame for the *Bounty* mutiny, Bligh was unlikely to suffer any officially sanctioned public disgrace because of his social status and the fact that Joseph Banks, one of the richest and most influential men in England, was his patron. He was given an unconditional, honourable acquittal and was promoted to post-captain soon after. Banks was sympathetic to Bligh's explanations for the mutiny and impressed by his seamanship and discipline in bringing the launch and those onboard to safety in Timor. Banks continued his support for Bligh by funding him to start preparations for a new voyage to transplant breadfruit.

In August 1791, Bligh took command of the *Providence* and her tender *Assistant*, and set sail once more for Tahiti. This time the voyage was a triumph and Bligh collected over 1000 healthy plants, delivering them in good condition to the planters in the West Indies,

Breadfruit trees can reach 18 metres in height

who presented him with a commemorative silver plate valued at 100 guineas. In addition, the Jamaican House of Assembly voted to pay him 1000 guineas. When he returned to England from Jamaica in 1793, Bligh's successful mission to transplant the breadfruit was rewarded with a gold medal by the Royal Society of Arts.

In one of the characteristic ironies associated with Bligh's expedition, the slaves working in the West Indian plantations refused to eat the transplanted breadfruit, seeing the imported and unfamiliar food as a symbol of their servitude, and it was not until 45 years later that they would willingly consider consuming it. In 1838, they achieved emancipation and began to eat the breadfruit, recognising it as the staple food of the West Indies and enjoying its nutritional values.

While Bligh was completing his breadfruit undertaking, the official version of the *Bounty*'s adventure was published in London as *A Voyage to the South Sea*. It was no unbiased account and was based heavily on Bligh's notebook and the *Bounty* logbook that he had with him on the launch. Also in this year of 1792, Captain Edward Edwards of HMS *Pandora* arrived in England with 10 of the mutineers retrieved from Tahiti. The story of the *Pandora* is as extraordinary as that of the *Bounty*.

A letter written on 10 July 1792 by a neighbour of Peter Heywood's mother to John Fryer, protesting the innocence of Heywood, who was facing court martial for his part in the mutiny

Edwards' one serious failure was the loss of the tender which was accompanying him. He spent a month trying to locate the missing schooner, which had become separated from the *Pandora* in the darkness on 22 June off Upolu, an island in Samoa. The other oversight occurred on 14 August when he sailed past an island, which he named Pitt Island, at the southernmost tip of the Solomon Islands. Edwards sailed within a mile of the reef that fringed the island and noticed that there were fires, indicating that the island was inhabited. He did not investigate further but, if he had, he may well have discovered the last two survivors of La Perouse's expedition, which had disappeared in 1788. Much later, investigation revealed that the two wrecks from that expedition lay under the water, victims of the same reef that Edwards had noticed and avoided.

On 28 August, the *Pandora* approached the Great Barrier Reef, and Edwards turned south to seek an entrance. He sent a boat to examine what appeared to be an opening in the reef. The sailing officer eased the ship in closer while the exploratory boat returned, having found the necessary entry point but, at this point, the luck of the *Pandora* ran out. At 7.20 pm it struck

On the evening of 28 August 1791, the *Pandora* struck the reef near the entrance to Endeavour Straits and sank the following day

the submerged reef, the hold quickly filling with water. Panicking in the dark, the mutineers in their cage wrenched off their irons in readiness to swim for their lives. Edwards ordered the irons replaced, the guards doubled and threatened to shoot or hang them if any other attempt at freedom was observed.

Gradually the ship was lifted over the reef by the motion of the waves and into calmer waters. Pumping and frantic bailing continued all night, and guns and all disposable objects were heaved overboard, but it became clear that the ship could not be saved. Edwards instructed the crew to load the provisions into the boats and to cut adrift anything that would float so that, as the ship sank, the crew would find objects to cling to. At this late stage, Edwards ordered that the prisoners be brought onto the deck, several at a time. Muspratt, Skinner and Byrn were first and the door locked behind them. Morrison begged the armourer's mate to open the cage door as the ship began to sink and the sentries rolled into the sea. In a brave, desperate act, William Moulter, the boatswain's mate on the *Pandora*, hauled himself onto the roof of the cell, pulled open the bar and threw the hatch away before leaping into the waves. All but Hilbrant managed to get out before the ship sank.

The boats carried the survivors to the beach. In all, 31 of the ship's company and Hilbrant, Stewart, Sumner and Skinner were drowned. Eighty-nine crew and 10 mutineers survived. In a bizarre repetition of Bligh's journey in the open boat, Edwards found himself preparing his two remaining vessels for an attempt to reach Timor. On 31 August, they set out through isolated reefs to the Endeavour Straits, then through 1000 miles of open sea to Timor, suffering hunger, threats from hostile local inhabitants and acute dehydration in the scorching heat.

After a journey of 16 days, they arrived at Timor, and Edwards found passage to England on a Dutch vessel for his remaining crew, the mutineers and a group of escaped convicts from Port Jackson, who had also managed to reach Timor. The vanished tender and its entire crew were discovered in Samarang. All arrived in England by 19 June 1792. In the subsequent court martial, Edwards was exonerated for the loss of the *Pandora*.

Two days after the court martial, the trial of the mutineers began onboard HMS *Duke*. Bligh was away on the second breadfruit mission, placing those he had promised to speak for in grave jeopardy. The trial is a depressing record of verdicts of guilt and innocence based on the social status and the ability, or inability, of the accused to pay lawyers. Heywood, who was extremely well connected through Commodore Pasley and other family networks, was sentenced to death but pardoned, as was Morrison. Muspratt was saved on a legal technicality. The remaining three men, Ellison, Millward and Burkitt—who had no wealth, no social position, no powerful patron to support their plea and no capacity to employ legal aid—were hanged ceremonially on HMS *Brunswick* in a very public spectacle. Perhaps most poignant is the hanging of Ellison, a boy of 16 when the mutiny occurred, who had been instructed by Bligh to take the helm, and had done so. By sticking to his post, he signed his death warrant. Ellison wrote his statement to the court martial, and this action of writing was entirely due to Bligh and his secretary teaching him to write on the *Bounty*. In the statement, he recreated the confusion of the scene with Christian wielding his weapons in the half-light of dawn: 'He looked like a Madman, is long hair was luse, is shirt collair open'. Ellison was fully sensible of the privilege of his lessons with Bligh:

> *I must have been very Ingreatfull if I had in any respect assisted in this Unhappy Affair agains my Commander and Benefactor, so I hope, honorable Gentlemen, yo'll be so Kind as to take my Case into Consideration as I was No more than between Sixteen and Seventeen Years of age when this of done.*

The court did not show mercy to this young man.

When Bligh returned from his second breadfruit mission, he found that his reception was cooler than he had expected, as the trial of the mutineers had attracted public attention, and Morrison's evidence and Heywood's correspondence with his family had brought to light evidence that showed Bligh's behaviour in a damaging light. On leaving the *Providence*, Bligh was discharged and placed on half pay, remaining unemployed until 29 April 1795. Fletcher Christian's brother, Edward, did not remain silent about the mutiny and, in 1794, published excerpts from the mutineers' court martial with an appendix arguing a defence of his brother.

Five years later, in 1797, many of the ships' companies, who had watched the execution of the *Bounty* mutineers, were part of major mutinies at Spithead and Great Nore, in which they protested violently at the appalling conditions for sailors on naval vessels. The mutiny on the *Bounty* had helped focus the attention of sailors on the injustices and brutalities of naval command and had fuelled the discontent that would erupt in these insurrections.

house Pitcairns Is.

Christian's house on Pitcairn Island

Fletcher Christian

And what became of Fletcher Christian and the men who remained with him as he searched for the ideal place to remain hidden from the British navy and establish a new life?

In 1808, an American seal-hunting ship, the *Topaz*, visited Pitcairn Island and found one mutineer alive—John Adams (Alexander Smith)—amidst nine Tahitian women. There were also children who were the offspring of the mutineers and their Tahitian wives. Adams explained that Christian had married the daughter of chief Maimiti in 1789 and had fathered three children with her: Thursday October Christian, Charles Christian and Mary Ann Christian. Christian had abandoned an attempt to establish a community on Tubuai Island, 400 miles south of Tahiti, after conflict with the local population and had sailed on to Pitcairn after leaving 16 crewmen on Tahiti. Both Adams and Maimiti explained that Christian had been killed by Tahitian men as he was gardening with his wife, who was pregnant with their daughter. Adams told of the brutal end for the other

Pitcairn Islanders, 1857—standing back row: Denise Young, Jane Nobbs, Miriam Christian, Dinah Quintal; seated middle row: Rebecca Evans, Ellen Quintal, Anne Naomi Nobbs, Jemima Young; standing left: George Parkyn (?) Christian; sitting on floor: Victoria Quintal, Sarah

POLLY ADAMS AND SISTERS
PITCAIRN ISLANDERS

Above: Pitcairn Islanders Polly Adams and her sisters, 1850s; Below: John Adams' house on Pitcairn Island

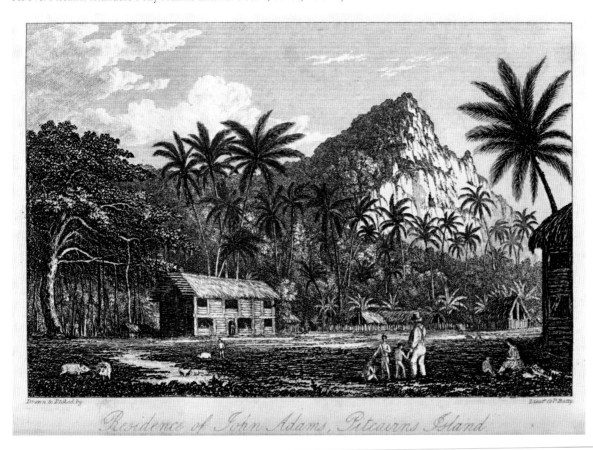

Residence of John Adams, Pitcairns Island

mutineers: four mutineers and six Tahitian men had died in the conflict erupting over the sexual imbalance in the community and the way in which the mutineers expected the Tahitian men to act as slaves; one mutineer fell off a cliff while intoxicated; and Quintal was killed by two remaining mutineers when he attacked them. This was no Pacific utopia.

Bligh's governorship

Just before his fifty-second birthday, on 13 August 1806, William Bligh found himself back in the Southern Hemisphere, taking office as fourth governor of New South Wales. Like Hunter and King before him, Bligh was shocked by the condition of the colony, writing that 'in the customs and manners of the people much was to be corrected'. The unfolding events leading to the rebellion of 1808 had their foundation in political and interpersonal dynamics as complex as those contributing to the mutiny on the *Bounty*, and the topic is worthy of a book in itself. Once again, Bligh's volatile temperament precipitated a crisis that resulted in his loss of authority. His orders were to administer the penal colony, in which he had supreme authority. The non-indigenous population of New South Wales consisted of 6935 people: 1380 convicts, 66 civil officials, 685 members of the New South Wales Corps and the rest civilian residents. From the 1790s, under the governments of Francis Grose and William Paterson, both of whom served under Arthur Phillip and John Hunter, the officers had exploited the potential of the new colony for capitalist ventures. Officers had received large land grants, along with convicts to work the land.

A fine example of the kind of self-made man who benefited from a career in the New South Wales Corps was Englishman John Macarthur, who had secured a posting as a lieutenant with the corps, arriving in Sydney in 1790. Governor Philip Gidley King writes of Macarthur:

> *His employment during the eleven years he has been here has been that of making a large fortune, helping his brother officers to make small ones (mostly at the publick expense) and sowing discord and strife.*

Macarthur, with his ambitions of establishing a wool industry in the colony, was destined to have a stormy relationship with Bligh, as Joseph Banks, Bligh's patron, had visions of an English company developing this opportunity. It must be noted that the governors themselves, including William Bligh, were involved in their own versions of private enterprise in the colonies. Before Bligh took up office as New South Wales governor, he accepted three land grants from Governor King, totalling 1345 acres. One thousand acres on the Hawkesbury

John Macarthur's residence near Parramatta, New South Wales

River were farmed by Bligh for private gain and he allocated himself convicts and animals, and erected buildings paid for by the government. A more politically astute man would have recognised that his acquisitive behaviour was not a good example with which to support his claims of moral superiority when he set about dismantling the financial privileges enjoyed by the New South Wales Corps. However, as we have seen in the discussion of the mutiny on the *Bounty*, tact and diplomatic skill were not Bligh's strengths.

By 1806, the emancipist merchants had broken the monopoly on trading in New South Wales. Financial benefits had also filtered down to reach the ranks of the corps. Many people in the colony in the late-eighteenth century saw the possibility of making their fortune through farming and commercial ventures, and there was bound to be conflict with governors who tried to obstruct this ambition.

Soon after taking up his post, Bligh replaced most of the existing officials with new appointments—an unpopular action in such a small community. Appalled at what he saw as the lamentable state of civic development, Bligh stated that he wanted to return to Governor Phillip's plans for Sydney, and he used this as the excuse for claiming that all town leases were legally invalid. In a public, theatrical clash, Macarthur debated his rights to a lease on Church Hill, fuelling fear in the other settlers and the corps that their land was about to be repossessed. In the tightly interconnected New South Wales community, residents became aware that in Bligh's dispatch to London on the state of the colony on 31 October 1807, he had suggested that regiments be rotated more often to prevent them from becoming entrenched in the local population and forming 'improper connections with women, by whom they have a number of children, and which lessens the respect due to the virtuous mothers and their families'. In Sydney, the New South Wales Corps accounted for 10 per cent of the population. The soldiers regarded themselves as permanent residents, not transient appointees like Bligh and, of about the 300 who lived in the town, only 120 lived

in the barracks. The corps' commander, George Johnston, wrote to the commander-in-chief of the British army, the Duke of York, to protest about the lack of dignity with which Bligh treated members of the corps. Johnston had a powerful civilian ally in John Macarthur, a one-time member of the corps, who had fought the attempts of previous governors Hunter and King to curb the entrepreneurial ventures of the corps and free settlers.

Bligh's behaviour in the *Bounty* mutiny did not help instil popular confidence in his appointment as governor. As a result of campaigns by Fletcher Christian's brother and other supporters to clear the name of the mutineers and justify their actions, public comment circulated that Bligh's unreasonable and dictatorial behaviour was responsible for the mutiny and rendered him unfit to govern in New South Wales. Letters condemning Bligh's 'violent, rash and tyrannical' temperament were written by Mrs John Macarthur, Lieutenant William Minchin, surgeon to the corps John Harris and avaricious landowner John Blaxland. In an early exercise in colonial anti-establishment political propaganda, the popular press circulated a verse in October 1807:

> *Oh tempora! Oh Mores! Is there*
> *no Christian in New South Wales to put*
> *a stop to the Tyranny of the Governor.*

In December 1807, events conspired that would make Bligh, now nick-named Caligula by some Sydney residents, the object of the 1808 mutiny. Bligh's radical changes to the grounds of government house were resented by sections of colonial society as he erased all evidence of a young soldier's tomb. All wandering dogs were ordered to be shot. In behaviour that was very different to the clemency that he had advocated when embarking on the *Bounty* voyage, Bligh's extreme reluctance to use his power as governor to pardon condemned prisoners was criticised and his abominable temper was despised. In a similar manifestation of the fury unleashed at Fletcher Christian just prior to the mutiny on the *Bounty*, on 28 September 1807, Bligh railed that 'vile wretches of soldiers laughed at his daughter in church that Sunday', ignoring Lieutenant Minchin's explanation that the laughter was directed at a drummer putting a feather in a cap. Bligh reacted furiously at what he interpreted as an insult, remarking that 'they might as well say the drummer had put a feather into the man's …… !'

Despite his volatile temper, Bligh had many supporters, but his undoing came when first he prosecuted Simeon Lord and his business associates in August 1807, then dismissed D'Arcy Wentworth from his role of assistant surgeon to the colony before turning his attention to bringing down Macarthur. Macarthur refused to pay a £900 bond that the government

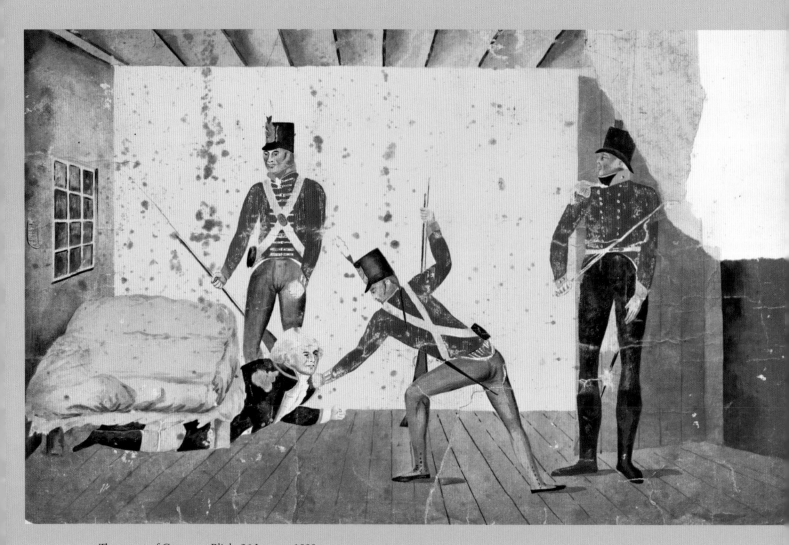

The arrest of Governor Bligh, 26 January 1808

demanded because a convict had escaped on a ship he owned. The grazier declined to offer a statement to legal authorities and he was ordered to appear in court. He would not 'submit to the horrid tyranny' and was arrested, eventually appearing in court on 25 January 1808. Macarthur protested against Richard Atkins, known for his drunken incompetence, acting as judge advocate, and appealed to the corps for their support. Johnston went to the barracks and declared himself lieutenant-governor, signing an order directing the keeper of His Majesty's gaol in Sydney to deliver John Macarthur to the men who had provided bail. Macarthur wrote a letter to Johnston that would topple Bligh once again from his position of righteous authority:

> *Sir,*
>
> *The present alarming state of this colony, in which every man's property, liberty and life is endangered, induces us most earnestly to implore you instantly to place Governor Bligh under an arrest and to assume the command of the colony. We pledge ourselves, at a moment of less agitation, to come forward to support the measure with our fortunes and our lives.*
>
> > *We are, with great respect, Sir,*
> >
> > *Your most obedient servants*
> >
> > | | |
> > |---|---|
> > | *Jno. Macarthur* | *Gregory Blaxland* |
> > | *Jno. Blaxland* | *James Badgery* |
> > | *James Mileham* | *Nicholas Bayly* |
> > | *S. Lord* | |

Johnston delivered the ultimate insult by writing to Bligh that he had been charged by the 'most respectable inhabitants of crimes that rendered him unfit to exercise the supreme authority for another moment in the colony' and that the governor must submit to arrest. These 'respectable inhabitants' were regarded by Bligh as base villains who threatened the Royal authority invested in him.

In the early evening of 26 January, hundreds of soldiers of the New South Wales Corps marched to government house with fixed bayonets as the band played 'British Grenadiers'. Bligh was confined to government house for a year, refusing to sail for England until officially relieved of command. He finally complied with Johnston's order, but sailed to Hobart instead, where he tried, unsuccessfully, to enlist the support of Lieutenant-Governor David Collins.

Throughout this time of imprisonment and disgrace, Bligh continued to write tirades to his friends in England about his enemies and rail against his opponents whenever an opportunity arose. Throughout his detention, he alienated most of the influential people he came in contact with by being arrogant and abusive. He returned to Sydney in January 1810 to find that the new governor, Lachlan Macquarie, had been installed. Macquarie found Bligh a most unpleasant nuisance in Sydney, abhorring his predecessor's temperament as abrasive and lacking social grace. In his investigations, Macquarie could find no actual crime or brutality committed by Bligh to justify, in any way, the rebellion of those who had arrested him and undermined his government. However, Macquarie believed that Bligh was universally hated by the population and that his temperament rendered him incapable of fulfilling his duties appropriately.

Bligh sailed for England in May, a little over a year after Johnston and Macarthur had sailed there to give their defence in the legal proceedings relating to the rebellion. Johnston was court-marshalled and dismissed from the corps. Macarthur, as a civilian, could not be tried for treason but was exiled until 1817, when he received permission to return provided he kept out of public affairs.

On Bligh's return to England, he was promoted to rear-admiral of the Blue, followed by rear-admiral of the White in 1812. In 1814, having received his pension the year before, he gained the high ranking of vice-admiral of the Blue. He died three years later. While there is much about breadfruit on Bligh's tomb in Lambeth churchyard, there is no mention of his term as governor of New South Wales. There were chapters in his life that William Bligh was happy to forget. The first mutiny was lamentable but was exonerated by Bligh's heroic voyage in the open launch. A second mutiny, however, was not an event to record on the tombstone of a vice-admiral of the Blue.

Perhaps the last word about Bligh after his disastrous colonial experience is best left to Manning Clark:

> Bligh continued to get on in the world while that other satisfaction he craved, getting on with the world, eluded him as unmistakably as ever.

Rear-Admiral William Bligh, 1814

List of mutineers

Facsimile and transcript

Fletcher Christian. Aged 24 Years — 5. 9 feet In High — Dark Swarthy Complexion

Complexion ——— Dark & very swarthy

Hair ——— Blackish or very dark brown

Make ——— Strong

Marks ——— Star tatowed on the left breast tatowed and on the backside. — His knees stands a little out, and may be called a little bow legged. He is subject to violent perspiration & particularly in His hands so that he soils any thing he handles.

George Stewart — Aged 23 — 5. 7 feet In High —

Complexion ——— Good

Hair ——— Dark

Make ——— Slender, narrow chested & long necked

Marks — Star on the left breast — one on the left Arm — tatowed on the backside — & tattooed with Darts on the left arm ——— Small face & black eyes

Peter Heywood ——— Aged 17 — 5. 7

Complexion ——— Fair

Hair —— Dark light brown

Make ——— Well proportioned

Marks ——— Very much tattowed and on the right Leg is tattowed the Three legs of Man as that coin is — At this time he had not done growing — He speaks with the Manks or Isle of Man accent

Edward Young ——— Aged 22. 5. 8 feet high

Complexion ——— Dark and a rather a bad look

Hair — — — Dark brown

Make ——— Strong

Marks ——— Lost several of his fore teeth & those that remain are all rotten. — A small mole on the left side of the throat and on the right arm is tatowed a heart & Dart through it with E. Y. underneath. and the year 1788 or 1789 feet In

Fletcher Christian. Aged 24 Years—5 .. 9 High Dark Swarthy Complexion
Complexion ————————Dark & very swathy
Hair————————————Blackish or very dark brown
Make————————————Strong
Marks —————————————Star tatowed on the left breast and tatowed on the
backside.—His knees stands a little out and may be called a little bow legged
He is subject to violent perspiration & particularly in His hands so that he
soils any thing he handles.

ft In

George Stewart—Aged 23—5 .. 7—High—
Complexion ————————Good
Hair————————————Dark
Make————————————Slender & narrow chested & long kneck
Marks —————————————Star on the left breast—one on the left Arm—
tatowed on the backside—A Heart with Darts on the left arm—Small face
& black Eyes.

f   in

Peter Haywood—Aged 17—5 .. 7
Complexion ————————Fair
Hair————————————Light brown
Make————————————well proportioned
Marks —————————————Very much tattowed and on the Right Leg is tattowed
The Three legs of Man as that coin is. At this time he had not done
growing—He speaks with Strong Manks or I. of Man accent

f   in

Edward Young—Aged 22 .. 5 .. 8 High
Complexion ————————Dark and rather a bad look
Hair_____Dark brown
Make————————————Strong
Marks —————————————Lost several of his fore teeth & those that remain are
all rotten.—A small mole on the left side of the throat and on the right arm is
tatowed [a?] Heart & Dart through it with E . Y underneath. and the
[date of?] the year 1788 or 1789.

Cha.ˢ Churchill – Aged 30 Years – 5..10 High

Complexion ——— fair

Hair .. ——— Short Light Brown. Top of the Head. Bald

Make ——— Slender –

Marks ——— has the Fore Finger of his left hand
crooked – and his hand shews the Marks of a Severe Scald.
Tatowed in several places of his Body. Legs & Arms –

James Morrison ——— Aged 28 Years – 5..8

Complexion ——— Sallow

Hair ..——— Long black Hair

Make ——— Slender

Marks ——— Lost the Use of the Upper Joint of the Fore
Finger of the Right Hand – Tatowed with a Star under his left
Breast & a Garter round his Left Leg with the Motto of
Soit Qui Mal y Pense – has been Wounded in One of his Arms with a
Musquet Ball.

John Mills .. ——— Aged 40 Years – 5..10

Complexion – fair

Hair ——— Light Brown

Make ——— Strong. Raw Boned.

Marks ——— Scar in his Right Arm Pit –

John Millward ——— Aged 22 Years – 5..5. High

Complexion ——— Brown

Hair ——— Dark –

Make ——— Strong –

Marks ——— Very much Tatowed in Diff.ᵗ parts and
is tatowed with the Pit of the Stomach with a Taoomy or Breast plate
of Otaheite –

                                    ft   In
Chas Churchill. Aged. 30 Years—5 .. 10 High
Complexion ——————fair
Hair ————————Short Light Brown. Top of the Head Bald
Make ——————Strong
Marks ——————The Fore Finger of his left hand Crooked—and his hand
shows the Marks of a Severe Scald. Tatowed in several places of the Body, Legs
& Arms—

James Morrison—Aged 28 Years— 5 .. 8
Complexion ——————Sallow
Hair————————Long Black Hair
Make————————Slender
Marks ——————Lost the Use of the Upper Joint of the Fore Finger of the
Right Hand—Tatowed with a Star under his left Breast & a Garter round his Left
Leg with the Motto of Honi Soit Qui Maly Pense.—has been Wounded in One of
his Arms with a Musquet Ball.

                                    f   i
John Mills—Aged 40 Years—5 .. 10
Complexion ——————fair
Hair————————Light Brown
Make ——————Strong. Raw Boned.
Marks ——————Scar in his Right Arm Pit—.

                                    ft   In
John Millward—Aged 22 Years—5—5 High
Complexion ——————Brown
Hair————————Dark
Make————————Strong
Marks ——————Very much Tatowed in Diff^t parts and is [marked in?] the
Pit of the Stomach with a Taoomy or Breastplate of Otaheite—

Math.w Thompson. Aged 40 Years — 5..8.

Complexion - - - Very Dark.

Hair ———— Short Black.

Make ———— Slender..—

Marks ———— Lost the Joint of the Great Toe of his Right

foot.—and is Tatowed in several Places —

W.m Mickoy. Aged 25 years —5..6 High

Complexion ——— Fair

Hair ——— Light Brown

Make ———— Strong —

Marks ———— A Scar where he has been Stabbd in the

Belly. and a Small Scar under his Chin — is Tatowed:

Math.w Quintal. —Aged 21 years 5..5

Complexion ——— Fair

Hair ——— Light Brown

Make ———— Strong

Marks ——— Very much tatowed on the Back Side

Legs & Arms & several other places

John Sumner ——— Aged 24 years —5..8. High

Complexion ——— Fair

Hair ——— Brown

Make ——— Slender

Marks ——— a Scar upon the left Cheek & tatowed

in several places

Tho.s Burkett - - - — Aged 26 years — 5..9 High

Complexion ——— Fair very much pitted with the Small Pox

Hair ——— Brown

Make ——— Slender

Marks ——— Very much tatowed.

```
                              ft  In
Mattʷ Thompson. Aged 40 Years—5 .. 8
Complexion ————————Very Dark
Hair————————————Short Black
Make————————————Slender
Marks ——————————————Lost the Joint of the Great Toe of his Right foot—and is
Tatowed in several places—


Wᵐ Mickoy  Aged 25 years—5 .. 6 High
Complexion ————————Fair
Hair————————————Light Brown
Make————————————Strong
Marks ——————————————A Scar where he has been Stabbed in the Belly. and a
Small Scar under his Chin—is Tatowed.


Mattʷ Quintal—Aged 21 years    5 .5
Complexion ————————Fair
Hair————————————Light Brown
Make————————————Strong
Marks ——————————————Very much tatowed on the Backside & several other places
Legs & Arms
                              ft  In
John Sumner—Aged 24 years—5 .. 8—High
Complexion ————————Fair
Hair————————————Brown
Make————————————Slender
Marks ——————————————A Scar upon the left Cheek & tatow in several places


Thoˢ Burkitt—Aged 26 years—5 .. 9 High
Complexion ————————fair very much pitted with the Small Pox
Hair————————————Brown
Make————————————Slender
Marks ——————————————Very much tatowed
```

Isaac Martin — Aged 30 Years 5.11 High

Complexion	Sallow
Hair	Light Brown
Make	Raw boned
Marks	Scars on the Left Breast —

Wm Musspratt — Aged 32 years — 5..6 High

Complexion	Darkish
Hair	Brown
Make	Slender
Marks	a Very Strong Black Beard. Scars under

his Chin Tatowed

Henry Hillbrant — Aged 25 years 5..7 High

Complexion	Sour
Hair	Sandy
Make	Strong
Marks	His Left Arm Shorter than the other

having been broke is a Hanoverian Born & Speaks Bad English

Allex Smith — Aged 22 years 5..5 High

Complexion	Brown
Hair	Brown
Make	Strong.
Marks	Very much pitted with the Small

Pox very much tatowed on his Body. Legs, Arms & feet
& as Scar on his Right foot where he has been Cut by a Wood 2 Axe

John Williams — Aged — 25 years 5..5 High

Complexion	Dark
Hair	Black
Make	Slender
Marks	has a Scar on the back part of the head and is a Native of Guernsey & Speaks French

Rich Skinner — Aged 22 Years — 5 — 8 High

Complexion	Fair
Hair	Light Brown
Make	Well Made
Marks	— Scars on both Ankles & on his Right Shin

Very much Tatowed by Trade a Hair Dresser

ft   In

Isaac Martin—Aged 30 years—5 .. 11 High

Complexion ————————Sallow

Hair————————Short Brown

Make————————Raw Boned

Marks ————————Star on the left Breast—

ft   In

Wᵐ Muspratt—Aged 30 years—5 .. 6 High

Complexion ————————Dark

Hair————————Brown

Make————————Slender

Marks ————————A Very Strong Black Beard. Scars under his Chin Tatowed

ft   In

Henʸ Hilbrant—Aged 25 years—5 .. 7 High

Complexion ————————fair

Hair————————Sandy

Make————————Strong

Marks ————————His Left Arm Shorter than the other having been broke—
is a Hanoverian Born & Speaks Bad English

ft   In

Alexʳ Smith—Aged 22 years   5 .. 5 High

Complexion ————————Brown

Hair————————Brown

Make————————Strong.

Marks ————————Very much pitted with the Small [Pox] & very much
tatowed on his Body, Legs, Arms & feet—& a Scar on his Right foot where he has
been cut by a Wood Ax

ft   In

John Williams—Aged—25 years   5 .. 5 High

Complexion ————————Dark

Hair————————Black

Make————————Slender

Marks ————————has a Scar on the back part of the head and is a Native of
Guernsey & Speaks French

ft   In

Richᵈ Skinner—Aged 22 years—5 .. 8 High

Complexion ————————Fair

Hair————————Light Brown

Make————————Well Made

Marks ————————Scars on both Ankles & on his Right Shin very much
tatowed by [trade?] a Hair Dresser

Michˢ Byrn — Aged 28 Years 5ft-6in High

Complexion ——— fair

Hair ——— Short fair

Make —— Slender

Marks ——— Almost Blind has the Marks of an Issue in
the Back of his Neck.

Thoˢ Ellison --- Aged 17 Years —— 5ft-3in

Complexion ——— fair

Hair ——— Dark

Make ——— Strong

Marks ——— Has got his Name Tatowed on his Right Arm
and Dated Octᵣ 25ᵗʰ 1708 —

Wᵐ Brown --—- Aged 27 Years — 5ft-8in High

Complexion ——— Fair

Hair ——— Dark Brown

Make ——— Slender

Marks —— A Remarkable Scar on one of his Cheeks

Which Contracts the Eye Lid and runs down to his throat Occasioned
by the Kings Evil — is Tatowed —

Joshᵗ Coleman — Armourer Aged 40 Years — 5ft-6in

Complexion ——— fair

Hair ——— Grey.

Make ——— Strong

Marks ——— & a Heart Tatowed on One of his Arms
and 1777 —

Thoˢ McIntosh - Carpˢ Crew — Aged 28 Years — 5ft-6in High

Complexion ——— Fair

Hair ——— Light Brown

Make ——— Slender

Marks --- —— pitted with the Small Pox

Robert Norman Carpˢ Mate — 26 Years — 5ft-9in

Complexion ——— fair

Hair ——— Light Brown

Make ——— Slender

Marks --- —— pitted with the Small Pox has a Remarkable
Motion with his head & Eyes ———

Turn Over.

```
                        ft  In
Mich¹ Byrn—Aged 28 years    5 .. 6 High
Complexion ————————fair
Hair————————————Short fair
Make————————————Slender
Marks ————————————Almost Blind has the Marks of an Issue in the Back of
his Neck.

                        ft  In
Thoˢ Ellison—Aged 17 years—5 .. 3
Complexion ————————fair
Hair————————————Dark
Make————————————Strong
Marks ————————————Has got his Name tatowed on his Right Arm and Dated
Octʳ 25ᵗʰ 1788—

                        ft  In
Wᵐ Brown—Aged 27 years—5 .. 8 High
Complexion ————————Fair
Hair————————————Dark Brown
Make————————————Slender
Marks ————————————A remarkable Scar on one of his Cheeks Which
Contracts the Eye Lid and runs down to his throat Occasioned by the
Kings Evil [=tuberculous swelling of the lymph glands in the neck]—
is Tatowed—

                        f   .
Josʰ Coleman Armourer—Aged 40 years—5 .. 6
Complexion ————————fair
Hair————————————Grey.
Make————————————Strong
Marks ————————————a Heart Tatowed on One of his [arms?] and 5777—

                        ft  In
Thoˢ Mᶜintosh—Carpˢ Mate—Aged. 28 years—5 .. 6 High
Complexion ————————Fair
Hair————————————Light Brown
Make————————————Slender
Marks ————————————pitted with the Small Pox

                        ft  In
Chaˢ Norman Carpˢ Mate—26 years—5 .. 9
Complexion ————————fair
Hair————————————Light Brown
Make————————————Slender
Marks ————————————pitted with the Small Pox has a Remarkable Motion
with his head and Eyes—
```

Turn Over

These — Joseph Coleman, Mich. Byrne, Thos. McIntosh and Chas. Norman are deserving of Mercy being detained against their inclinations. —

These—Joseph Coleman Mich^l Byrne—Thos McIntosh and Chas Norman are deserving of mercy being detained against their inclinations.—

Wm Bligh

The Bounty crew at the time of the mutiny

In the Royal Navy, there were commissioned officers who received their commission from the Admiralty, and there were warrant officers who received their warrant from the Navy Board.

The loyalists

Lieutenant William Bligh, commander and purser (the only commissioned officer)

John Fryer, master (warrant officer)

Thomas Ledward, acting surgeon (warrant officer)

David Nelson, botanist

William Peckover, gunner (warrant officer)

William Cole, boatswain (warrant officer)

William Purcell, carpenter (warrant officer)

William Elphinstone, master's mate

Thomas Hayward, midshipman

John Hallett, midshipman

John Norton, quartermaster

Peter Linkletter, quartermaster

Lawrence Lebogue, sail maker

John Smith, cook

Thomas Hall, cook

George Simpson, quartermaster's mate

Robert Tinkler, a boy

Robert Lamb, butcher

John Samuel, clerk

The mutineers

Fletcher Christian, master's mate

Peter Heywood, midshipman

George Stewart, midshipman

Edward Young, midshipman

Charles Churchill, master-at-arms

John Mills, gunner's mate

James Morrison, boatswain's mate

Thomas Burkitt, able seaman

Matthew Quintal, able seaman

John Sumner, able seaman

John Millward, able seaman

William McCoy, able seaman

Henry Hilbrant, able seaman

William Muspratt, able seaman

Alexander Smith (John Adams), able seaman

John Williams, able seaman

Thomas Ellison, able seaman

Isaac Martin, able seaman

Richard Skinner, able seaman

Matthew Thompson, able seaman

William Brown, botanist's assistant

Michael Byrn, able seaman

Joseph Coleman, armourer

Charles Norman, carpenter's mate

Thomas McIntosh, carpenter's crew

Glossary of nautical terms

able seaman	an experienced deckhand who could carry out routine duties
aft	at the back of a vessel
armourer	the ship's gunsmith, blacksmith and metalworker
binnacle	housing for the ship's compass, placed where it could be seen by the man at the wheel
the Blue (vice-admiral of)	the Royal Navy used the colours red, white and blue to indicate an admiral's seniority, red being the highest rank
boatswain	the leading seaman in charge of the maintenance of the ship's equipment, especially the sails, rigging and hull
boatswain's mate	the assistant to the boatswain
carpenter	a man who maintained the ship's hull and masts
carvel construction	building hulls of vessels by fixing planks to each other so that they are joined flush at the seams, without overlaps
clinker construction	building hulls of vessels by fixing planks to each other so that they overlap along their edges
cutter	a single-masted sailing vessel
dead reckoning	navigating by calculating a position using the course, speed and time from a known position
departure	the distance sailed due east or west by a vessel on its course, the latitude and longitude of the point from which a vessel calculates dead reckoning
derrick	a lifting device composed of one mast or pole which is hinged freely at the bottom
fair journal	logbook
fairlead	a device, such as a ring, hole or hook, to guide a rope around an object or out of the way, or to stop the rope from moving laterally
foremast	the mast nearest the front or bow of a vessel
foremast-man	a man stationed to attend to the gear of the foremast
grapnel	a small anchor with three or four flukes, especially one used for anchoring a small vessel
gunner	a man who maintained a ship's guns
gunwale	the top edge of a boat's sides that forms a ledge around the whole boat above the deck
helm	a device, such as a wheel or tiller, used to steer a vessel
jolly boat	usually the smallest type of boat carried on a ship, with four or six oars; it could carry only a few people and was used to transport people and goods to and from shore, carry out inspections of the ship, or other small tasks
launch	the largest boat carried on a large ship and used for transport ashore, for small expeditions and as a lifeboat
log	a quadrant-shaped piece of wood, weighted on the rim to stand upright in the water, attached to the logline
logbook or log	the ship's record book or journal, containing entries for the weather, navigation data, watch keepers' names, sightings, and other significant information

logline	a line of determined length, knotted at regular intervals, with a piece of wood (the log) attached to its end, which is thrown over the stern to measure the ship's speed
lug sail	an irregularly shaped four-sided sail fixed to a beam that crosses the mast at an angle
master	shipmaster, able to command ships in non-combative situations, had navigational responsibilities
master's mate	the assistant to the master
master-at-arms	a man who maintained disciplinary regulations on a ship
meridians	an imaginary line between the north and south poles that crosses the equator at right angles. A meridian is designated by the degrees of longitude that it is west or east of the prime meridian at Greenwich, England
midshipman	an officer cadet of the lowest rank
packet	a boat or ferry carrying passengers, cargo and mail on regular short runs
purser	overseer of food supplies, clothing, bedding and other consumables
quadrant	instrument to measure angles and altitudes of stars, for navigation
quarterdeck	the rear part of the upper deck of a ship used by officers for official ceremonies and disciplinary hearings
quartermaster	the man who monitored the helmsman, assisted in some navigational duties and was responsible for signals
reefing the sails	shortening the sails in strong winds to decrease the power of the sail
rhumb line	a course line that follows the rhumb line intersects all meridians at the same angle
sail maker	maintained the sails and other canvas work
sextant	a navigational instrument with a telescope and an angular scale that is used to work out latitude and longitude—a celestial body is viewed through the telescope and its angular distance above the horizon is read off the scale; the data is then used to calculate the viewer's position.
shroud	supporting ropes or wires that extend from the top of a mast to the deck and which can be tightened to support the mast
sloop	a sailing vessel carrying a single mast mounted farther forward than the mast of a cutter
stern	the rear part of a ship
surgeon	the man who assisted the sick and injured, performed surgery, dispensed medicine
tender	a boat used to service a ship, by transporting people and/or supplies to and from shore or another ship
traverse tables	tables that enable the navigator to work out a new position by calculating the distance run from a known point and expressing the result in latitude and longitude
the White (rear-admiral of)	the Royal Navy used the colours red, white and blue to indicate an admiral's seniority, red being the highest rank
windlass	a winch

Page 74
William Bligh (1754–1817)
frontispiece reproduced from *Verhaal van de Muitery, an boord van het Engelsch Koningsschip de* Bounty ... by William Bligh (Dutch translation of *Narrative of the Mutiny on Board His Majesty's Ship Bounty* by Gerard Abraham Arrenberg, 1790)

Page 76
Jean-Francois de Galaup (1741–1788)
Carte d'une partie du Grand Ocean a l'E. et S.E. de la Nouvelle Guinee pour l'intelligence du voyage de la fregate espagnola la Princesa commandee par D. Franco. Antonio Maurelle en 1781 (detail) 1797
map; 31.4 x 46.8 cm
Maps Collection, nla.map-t1594

Page 77
Jacques Arago (1790–1855)
Vue de l'Ile Kandabou, Archipel des Viti 1833
plate 97 reproduced from *Voyage de la corvette l'Astrolabeexecute par ordre du Roi pendant les annees 1826–1827–1828–1829 sous le commandement de M. J. Dumont d'Urville* (Paris: J. Tastu, 1830–1834)
hand-coloured lithograph; 21.8 x 34.0 cm
Pictures Collection, nla.pic-an8264638

Page 78
Unknown artist
The Herald in Feejee 1850s
hand-coloured lithograph; 24.2 x 21.7 cm
Pictures Collection, nla.pic-an9537881

page 79
William Bligh (1754–1817)
A Chart of Bligh's Islands Discovered by Captain Wm. Bligh 1792?
hand-coloured manuscript map; 40.0 x 50.5 cm.
Maps Collection, nla.ms-ms6423-3x

Page 85
Arthur William Devis (1763–1822)
Portrait of Captain Wilson of Antelope (detail) c.1782
oil on canvas; 74.0 x 60.8 cm
Pictures Collection, nla.pic-an2282361

Page 86
C. Essex & Co., London
Compass, Sundial and Geographical Clock c.1780
brass and wood; diam. 7 cm
Pictures Collection, nla.pic-an6561322

Page 87
William Bligh (1754–1817)
A Chart of Bligh's Straits in the Clarence Archipelago Discovered & Explored by Captain William Bligh of the Royal Navy 1792
coloured manuscript map; 36.3 x 48.4 cm
Manuscripts Collection, nla.ms-ms6423-1x

Page 88
William Watts
Pocket watch, c.1789
metal, enamel and glass; 7.2 x 5.1 x 2.7 cm
Courtesy National Maritime Museum, Greenwich, London

Page 94
William Dickinson (1746–1823)
Portrait of Joseph Banks Esq, 30 January 1774
mezzotint; 50.5 x 35.5 cm
Pictures Collection, nla.map-an9283218-1

Page 97
James Cook (1728–1779)
A Chart of the Southern Hemisphere: Shewing the Tracks of Some of the Most Distinguished Navigators 1777
map; diameter 49.5 cm
Maps Collection, nla.map-nk2456-15

Page 98
William Ellis (c.1756–1785)
View of Adventure Bay, Van Diemen's Land, New Holland 1777
watercolour and ink; 20.0 x 47.3 cm
Pictures Collection, nla.pic-an10345304

Page 99 (right)
Great Britain. Hydrographic Department (Edwd. Weller, lithographer)
South West Pacific: New Hebrides Islands, Banks Group: Sketch Survey by Lieutt. A.M. Field, R.N., and the Officers of H.M.S. Dart, 1886 1887
map; 66.1 x 48.5 cm
Maps Collection, nla.map-rm1823

Page 104
E. Whimper
The Flying Fish, Exocetus volitans c.1850
hand-coloured engraving; 27.6 x 34.2 cm
Pictures Collection, nla.pic-vn403594

Page 106
James M. Norton
A model of the *Bounty* launch, 2003
basswood, linen, polymer clay and acrylic paint
33.0 x 10.1 x 21.6 cm (scale 1:24)
Courtesy James M. Norton

Page 107
The horn beaker Bligh used to measure the daily water allowance
5.4 x 4.8 cm
Courtesy National Maritime Museum, Greenwich, London

Page 109
Unknown artist
Illustrations of waterspouts, and an eclipse, 1830 (detail)
plate reproduced from *Narrative of a Voyage to the Pacific and Beering's Strait* by Frederick William Beechey (London: Henry Colburn & Richard Bentley, 1830)
aquatint; 10.0 x 17.5 cm
Pictures Collection, nla.pic-an10243109

Page 114
The coconut bowl on which Bligh carved his name, the date and the words: 'the cup I eat my miserable allowance out of', 1789 (detail)
10.2 x 12.7 cm
Courtesy National Maritime Museum, Greenwich, London

Page 115
The bullet pendant that Bligh used as a weight to measure the men's daily ration of bread, 1789
6.3 x 3.5 x 1.0 cm
Courtesy National Maritime Museum, Greenwich, London

Page 116
Henry Constantine Richter (1821–1902)
Thalissodroma melanogaster, *Black-bellied Storm Petrel* 1847
watercolour; 38.37 x 54.5 cm
Pictures Collection, nla.pic-an10049028

Page 117
See caption for page 114 above

Page 122
Great Britain. Hydrographic Department
Chart of Part of the N.E. Coast of Australia: Sheet 3 by Phillip P. King, Commander, R.N., 1819, 20, 21; with Additions by Lieut. Roe, R.N. 1829 and by Captain F.P. Blackwood, R.N. 1844
map; 80.6 x 50.9 cm
Maps Collection, nla.map-vn3791275

Page 124
John Fryer (1752–1817)
A page from the original manuscript of 'Narrative of the mutiny on HMS *Bounty* and the voyage in the Bounty launch'
Courtesy Mitchell Library, State Library of New South Wales

Page 125
Gurtano Calleja
Portrait of John Fryer between 1787 and 1817
oil; 69.0 x 53.5 cm
Courtesy Mitchell Library, State Library of New South Wales

Page 132
Unknown artist
The Kanguroo
reproduced from *Dangerous Voyage of Captain Bligh in an Open Boat over 1200 Leagues of the Ocean, in the Year 1789* by William Bligh (London: John Arliss, 1818)

Page 133
Detail of *Chart of Part of the N.E. Coast of Australia* (see caption for page 122 above)

Page 134
Unknown artist
Two Australian Natives on a Hill Throwing Their Weapons 1828?
watercolour; 18.0 x 22.8 cm
Pictures Collection, nla.pic-an6431245

Page 135
Marrianne Collinson Campbell (1827–1903)
Cissus antarctica, Billardiera longiflora *and* Syzygium austral 1800s
watercolour; 28.2 x 20.5 cm
Pictures Collection, nla.pic-vn3624612

Page 142
Unknown artist
Four Drawings of Islands off the East Coast of Australia (Forbes Island, Dunk Island, Holborne Island, Sunday Island) 1864
pencil; 27.8 x 20.2 cm
Pictures Collection, nla.pic-an5812818

Page 144
Detail from *The Mutineers Turning Lieut. Bligh and Part of the Officers and Crew Adrift from His Majesty's Ship the* Bounty (see caption for page 34 above)

Page 145
Pieter Bleeker (1819–1878)
Centrophorus moluccensis (Endeavour Dogfish)
figure 2a, plate 26, vol. 14, reproduced from facsimile edition of vols 11–14 of *Atlas ichthyologique des Indes orientales néêrlandaises: publié sous les auspices du gouvernement colonial néêrlandais* by P. Bleeker (Washington, D.C.: Smithsonian Institution, 1984)
Courtesy Smithsonian Institution

Page 152
Unknown artist
Captain Matthew Flinders, R.N. 1814
stipple engraving; 9.0 x 7.5 cm
Pictures Collection, nla.pic-an9455829-1

Page 153
Frontispiece and title page reproduced from *A Voyage to the South Sea Undertaken by Command of His Majesty, for the Purpose of Conveying the Bread-fruit Tree to the West Indies, in His Majesty's Ship the* Bounty ... by William Bligh (Dublin: P. Wogan, P. Byrne, W. M'Kenzie et al., 1792)

Page 158
Unknown artist
Hirundo or the Flying Fish c.1800
b&w engraving; 16.9 x 19.3 cm
Pictures Collection, nla.pic-vn4033802

Page 159
Table 20 copied from *Tables Requisite To Be Used with the Nautical Ephemeris for Finding the Latitude and Longitude at Sea* by Commissioners of Longitude (London: printed by William Richardson; and sold by C. Nourse, and Mess. Mount and Page, 1781)

Page 161
Henry Constantine Richter (1821–1902)
Attagen ariel, *Small Frigate Bird* 1848
watercolour; 38.3 x 55 cm
Pictures Collection, nla.pic-an10088496

Page 166
Charles Alexandre Lesueur (1778–1846)
Timor, vue de la rade, de la ville et du fort de Coupang (detail)
plate 39 reproduced from *Voyage de decouvertes aux terres australes* by François Péron (Paris: de l'Imprimerie de Langlois, 1807)
engraving; 24.0 x 49.0 cm
Pictures Collection, nla.pic-an7568625

Pages 168–169
See caption for page 166 above

Page 171
Unknown artist
The Gannet
reproduced from *Dangerous Voyage of Captain Bligh in an Open Boat over 1200 Leagues of the Ocean, in the Year 1789* by William Bligh (London: John Arliss, 1818)

Page 178
William Bromley (engraver, 1769–1842); Charles Benazech (artist, 1767–1794)
The Hospitable Behaviour of the Governor of Timor to Lieutenant Bligh 1802
engraving; 12.4 x 17.9 cm
Pictures Collection, nla.pic-an9455324

Page 179
Replica of the *Bounty*'s flag, which Captain Ware carried with him on the re-creation of Bligh's voyage in the *Bounty* launch in 1983
Manuscripts Collection, MS 5171

Page 180
J. Alphonse Pellion
Ile Timor, vue prise aux environs de Coupang 1819?
watercolour; 19.3 x 27.5 cm
plate 28 reproduced from *Voyage autour du monde ... 1817–1820. Atlas historique* by Louis de Freycinet (Paris, 1825)
Pictures Collection, nla.pic-an3099786

Page 183
Jean Nicolas Lerouge (1776–?)
Ile Timor, interieur d'une maison timorienne 1822?
hand-coloured stipple engraving; 23.2 x 31.0 cm
Pictures Collection, nla.pic-an9031336

Page 186
Homann Erben (Firm)
Der Hollaendisch-Ostindianischen Compagnie weltberuhmte Haupt-Handels und Niederlags-Stadt Batavia ... (Map of Batavia, now Jakarta, showing Dutch East India Company buildings, rice fields and canals)
plate 3 reproduced from *Stadt-Atlas, oder: Schauplatz beruhmter Stadte, Vestungen, Prospeckte, Gegenden, Grundrisse, Belagerungen ...* (Nurnberg, 1762)
colour map; 45.8 x 54.1 cm
Maps Collection, nla.map-rm270

Page 188
Unknown artist
Bread Fruit Tree 1830?
watercolour; 75.0 x 51.0 cm
Pictures Collection, nla.pic-an14124690

Page 191
J. Vose
Letter to John Fryer, 10 July 1792
Manuscripts Collection, MS 6591

Page 192
Lt-Col. Batty (1848–?) after sketch by Peter Heywood
etching
HMS Pandora *in the Act of Foundering*
reproduced from *The Eventful History of the Mutiny and Piratical Seizure of HMS* Bounty: *Its Cause and Consequences* by Sir John Barrow (London: John Murray, 1831)

Page 195
Conway Shipley (1824–?)
Christian's House, Pitcairn Island 1851
lithograph; 19.6 x 27.2 cm
Pictures Collection, nla.pic-an9947653

Page 196
Unknown photographer
Pitcairn Islanders, 1857
b&w photograph; 8.8 x 14.2 cm
Pictures Collection, nla.pic-vn3105785

Page 197 (top)
Unknown artist
Polly Adams and Sisters, Pitcairn Islanders 1850s
lithograph; 10.0 x 17.0 cm
Pictures Collection, nla.pic-an9281374

Page 197 (bottom)
Robert Batty (1848–?)
Residence of John Adams, Pitcairns Island
reproduced from *The Eventful History of the Mutiny and Piratical
Seizure of H.M.S.* Bounty: *Its Causes and Consequences* by Sir John
Barrow (London: John Murray, 1831)

Page 199
Joseph Lycett (c.1775–1828)
*The Residence of John McArthur Esqre. near Parramatta, New South
Wales* 1825
hand-coloured aquatint; 23.2 x 33 cm
Pictures Collection, nla.pic-an7690900

Page 202
Unknown artist
Arrest of Governor Bligh, January 26, 1808 1900s
colour illustration, facsimile; 27.0 x 44.0 cm
Pictures Collection, nla.pic-an7655522

Page 205
Alexander Huey (active 1809–1818)
Portrait of Rear-Admiral William Bligh 1814
watercolour on ivory; 11.5 x 8.4 cm
Pictures Collection, nla.pic-an11230917

Sources

Bach, John (ed.), *The Bligh Notebook: 'Rough Account—Lieutenant Wm Bligh's Voyage in the* Bounty*'s Launch from the Ship to Tofua & from Thence to Timor', 28 April to 14 June 1789, with a Draft List of the* Bounty *Mutineers*. Facsim. edn. Canberra: National Library of Australia, 1986.

Barrow, John Sir, *Mutiny! The Real History of the HMS* Bounty. New introduction by Edward E. Leslie. New York: Cooper Square Press, 2003. (Originally published as *Eventful History of the Mutiny and Piratical Seizure of H.M.S.* Bounty: *Its Causes and Consequences*. London: J. Murray, 1831.)

Bligh, William, *Account of the Mutiny on H.M. Ship* Bounty: *Addressed to Sir Joseph Bank*s. Edited, with an introduction and notes by John Currey. Malvern, Vic.: Colony Press, 2008.

Bligh, William, Notebook and List of Mutineers, 1789. National Library of Australia, Manuscripts Collection, MS 5393, http://nla.gov.au/nla.ms-ms5393.

Bligh, William, *The Log of H.M.S.* Bounty, *1787–1789*. Surrey, Eng.: Genesis Publications, 1975.

Bligh, William, *A Narrative of the Mutiny on Board His Majesty's Ship* Bounty: *And the Subsequent Voyage of Part of the Crew in the Ship's Boat, from Tofoa, One of the Friendly Islands, to Timor a Dutch Settlement in the East Indies*. Dublin: L. White, P. Byrne, J. Moore, J. Jones, B. Dornin, Grueber and M'Allister, W. Jones and R. White, 1790.

Bligh, William, *A Voyage to the South Sea: Undertaken by Command of His Majesty, for the Purpose of Conveying the Bread-fruit Tree to the West Indies, in His Majesty's Ship the* Bounty *Commanded by Lieutenant William Bligh … *. London: George Nicol, 1792.

Brunton, Paul (ed. and introduction), *Awake Bold Bligh! William Bligh's Letters Describing the Mutiny on HMS* Bounty. Sydney: Allen & Unwin and State Library of New South Wales, 1989.

Clark, C.M.H., *A History of Australia*, vol. 1. Carlton, Vic.: Melbourne University Press, 1962.

Commissioners of Longitude, *Tables Requisite To Be Used with the Nautical Ephemeris for Finding the Latitude and Longitude at Sea*. London: printed by William Richardson; and sold by C. Nourse, and Mess. Mount and Page, 1781.

Cook, James, *A Voyage to the Pacific Ocean: Undertaken by Command of His Majesty, for Making Discoveries in the Northern Hemisphere, Performed under the Direction of Captains Cook, Clerke, and Gore, in the Years 1776, 1777, 1778, 1779, and 1780 … *. London: John Stockdale, Scatcherd and Whitaker, John Fielding, and John Hardy, 1784.

Dening, Greg, *The* Bounty: *An Ethnographic History*. Parkville, Vic.: History Department, University of Melbourne, 1988.

Dening, Greg, *Mr Bligh's Bad Language: Passion, Power, and Theatre on the* Bounty. Cambridge, England; New York: Cambridge University Press, 1992.

Du Rietz, Rolf E., *The Bias of Bligh: An Investigation into the Credibility of William Bligh's Version of the* Bounty *Mutiny*. Uppsala, Sweden: Dahlia Books, 2003.

Fateful Voyage website. *The Mutiny on the Bounty: The Original Source Documents, All in One Place*. Viewed 22 April 2010 at www.fatefulvoyage.com/index.html.

Ford, Herbert, *The Mutiny's Cause: A New Analysis*. Pitcairn Islands Study Center, Pacific Union College, viewed 22 April 2010, at http://library.puc.edu/pitcairn/bounty/mutiny.shtml.

Fryer, John, *The Voyage of the* Bounty *Launch: John Fryer's Narrative; with an Introduction by Stephen Walters.* Adelaide: Rigby; Guildford, England: Genesis Publications, 1979.

Hainsworth, David Roger, *The Sydney Traders: Simeon Lord and His Contemporaries 1788–1821.* 2nd edn. Carlton, Vic.: Melbourne University Press, 1981.

Hamilton Moore, John, *The New Practical Navigator: Being an Epitome of Navigation.* Newburyport, Mass.: Edmund M. Blunt, 1799.

Lavery, Brian, *Nelson's Navy: The Ships, Men and Organisation 1793–1815.* London: Conway Maritime, 1990.

Nicol, Bill, *Timor: A Nation Reborn.* Jakarta: Equinox Publishing, 2002.

Mackaness, George (ed.), *A Book of the 'Bounty': William Bligh and Others.* London: J.M. Dent & Sons, 1938.

Mackaness, George, *The Life of Vice-Admiral William Bligh.* New and revised edn. Sydney: Angus and Robertson, 1951.

Montgomerie, H.S., *The Morrison Myth: A Pendant to William Bligh of the* Bounty *in Fact and in Fable.* London: H.S. Montgomerie, 1938.

Morrison, James, *The Journal of James Morrison, Boatswain's Mate of the* Bounty: *Describing the Mutiny & Subsequent Misfortunes of the Mutineers: Together with an Account of the Island of Tahiti.* Introduction by Owen Rutter and five engravings by Robert Gibbings. London: Golden Cockerel Press, 1935.

National Maritime Museum, *Mutiny on the* Bounty: *An International Exhibition to Mark the 200th Anniversary 28 April 1989–1 Oct 1989.* London: Manorial Research PLC in association with the National Maritime Museum, 1989.

Rutter, Owen, *Turbulent Journey: A Life of William Bligh, Vice-Admiral of the Blue.* London: Ivor Nicholson, 1936.

State Library of New South Wales, *Mutiny on the* Bounty: *The Story of Captain William Bligh, Seaman, Navigator, Surveyor and of the* Bounty *Mutineers.* Sydney: State Library of New South Wales, 1998.

Toohey, John, *Captain Bligh's Portable Nightmare.* New York: HarperCollinsPublishers, 2000.

Wahlroos, Sven, *Mutiny and Romance in the South Seas: A Companion to the* Bounty *Adventure.* Topsfield, Mass.: Salem House Publishers, c.1989.

Index

Page numbers in **bold** refer to illustrations. Page numbers followed by N refer to extracts from Bligh's notebook.

232

Route of the *Bounty* launch, 1789

1 *Mutiny*: 28 April

2 *Tofua (landfall)*: 29 April

3 *Bligh's Islands (Fiji)*: 5–6 May

4 *Banks Islands (Vanuatu)*: 14 May

5 *Restoration Island (landfall)*: 29 May

6 *Sunday Island (landfall)*: 31 May

7 *Booby Island*: 4 June

8 *Coupang (landfall)*: 14 June